Socio-Historical Context of Paul's Confrontation in Galatians and Christian Identity in a Pluralistic Society

Biblical Hermeneutics Rediscovered

The Series as the name suggests will focus on Biblical Hermeneutics, i.e., literary works concerned with methods of interpreting the Old and New Testaments of Bible via different stream of topics like Literature & Poetry, Indigenous Philosophizing, Ethical response towards Ecology, Health & Healing, Science & Technology, Feminist Theology, Sociological approach towards Human Rights, Law & Politics, Arts, History of Ideas, Ancient Civilizations, Cultural Contiguity, Religious Cosmologies & Mysticism, Appraisal of various Theologians, World Peace & Harmony, Global Capitalism, Network Marketing, Cybertheology, Population & Demographics, Epigraphic Studies, Contextualized Education, and many others. We welcome a Mss. on any topic/s mentioned, whether they are original works, scholarly monographs, collections of conference papers, revised dissertations, or translations of historical documents. Through the Series we, the Publishers, are striving to put forward published works that may help Institutions, Academic Bodies, Researchers, Scholars and the World at large in furthering their respective knowledge and understanding on the concerned subject. We welcome your comments on our efforts and further suggestions on how we can enshrine new ray of analysing & explaining the written Texts through our upcoming books.

Biblical Hermeneutics Rediscovered - 5

Socio-Historical Context of Paul's Confrontation in Galatians and Christian Identity in a Pluralistic Society

Ashok Ram Rana

CWI

Christian World Imprints(TM)

First Published in 2017 by

Christian World Imprints(TM)
Christian Publishing & Books from India
H-12 Bali Nagar, **New Delhi-110015**
info@christianworldimprints.com
www.ChristianWorldImprints.com
Phone: +91 11 25465925

ISBN: 978-93-5148-192-8 (HB)   ISBN: 978-93-5148-193-5 (PB)

Cataloging in Publication Data--DK
Courtesy: D.K. Agencies (P) Ltd. <docinfo@dkagencies.com>

Rana, Ashok Ram, 1981- **author.**
Socio-historical context of Paul's confrontation in Galatians and Christian identity in a pluralistic society / Ashok Ram Rana.
pages cm. -- (Biblical hermeneutics rediscovered ; 5)
Includes bibliographical references.
ISBN 9789351481928 (HB)
ISBN 9789351481935 (PB)

1. Bible. Galatians.--Criticism, interpretation, etc. 2. Identification (Religion) 3. Religious pluralism--Christianity. 4. Christianity--India. I. Title. II. Series: Biblical hermeneutics rediscovered ; 5.

BS2685.52.R36 2017   DDC 227.406 23

Printed in India.

Dedicated
to My Parents

Contents

Foreword xiii
Abstract xv
Acknowledgment xvii
Introduction xix

Chapter 1: Historical and Socio-Cultural Context of Paul's Confrontation in Galatians 1
Introduction 1
1.1 Destination of Galatians 2
1.2 Confrontation 3
1.3 Historical Account of Confrontation in Biblical History 3
1.3.1 Prophetic Movement as an Example of Confrontation 4
1.3.2 Confrontation During Maccabean Revolt 5
1.3.3 The Letter of Aristeas 10
1.3.4 Confrontation in the Gospels and Paul's Letters 11
1.4 Social Sciences and Galatians' Context 12
1.5 Religious-Political and Socio-Cultural Issues in Galatians 16
1.5.1 Conversion 16
1.5.2 Eating Together and Converts' Fellowship 17
1.5.3 James' Impact on Peter's Withdrawal 18
1.5.4 Jewish Purity Requirement 18

1.6 The Concept of Ecclesiology in Paul 19
1.6.1 Greaco-Roman World 20
1.6.2 έκκλησία 21
1.6.3 Purpose of έκκλησία 22
1.6.3.1 Paul's Usage 22
1.6.3.2 Church as Gathering 23
1.6.4 Metaphor of έκκλησία 24
1.6.4.1 Building 24
1.6.4.2 Temple of God 25
1.6.4.3 *Soma*: Body of Christ 25
1.6.4.3.1 An Ecclesial Christology 26
1.6.4.3.1.1 You are Christ's Body 26
1.6.4.3.1.2 Christ, the Head of the Body-Church 27
1.6.4.3.2 Building up the Body of Christ 28
1.7 Jerusalem Council and Its Impact on Galatians Christian Community 29
1.7.1 Arguments for the Identity Between Galatians 2:1-10 and Acts 15 30
1.7.2 Similarity in People and Issues 30
1.7.3 Paul as the Apostle to the Gentiles 31
1.7.4 A Literary Argument 32
1.7.5 Galatians and Romans 33
1.7.6 Εσπούδασα in Galatians 2:10 33
1.7.7 Two Objections 34
1.8 Arguments for the Identity Between Galatians 2:1-10 and Acts 11:27-30 and 12:25 34
1.8.1 Paul and the Incident with Peter 35
1.8.2 Paul's Work in Syria and Cilicia 35
1.8.3 Two Objections 35
1.9 Paul's Experience: Conversion or Call? 37
Summary 38

Chapter 2: Socio-Cultural Approach to Galatians 2 and Other Related Texts 41

Introduction 41

2.1 Paul's Argument and its Context in Gal: 1:1-11 42

2.1.1 Paul's defending of his Apostleship against Agitators 42

2.1.2 Argument No: 2 Paul's warning "Not to accept the different Gospel" (VV. 6-10) 45

2.1.3 The Reasons for Paul Astonishment 46

2.1.4 The Characterization of the False Teachers' Message 47

2.1.5 Characterization of the Paul's Message 47

2.2 Paul's Exposure of Peter's Eating Habits (vv 11-14a) 48

2.3 Paul's Response to Peter's Attitude (vv 14b-21) 56

2.4 Historical Analysis of the Incident at Antioch 60

2.5 Evaluation of Texts 62

2.5.1 Paul's Second Visit to Jerusalem (Gal 2: 1-10) 62

2.5.2 A Betrayal of the Gospel of Christ 63

2.5.3 Pauline View of Freedom 64

2.5.4 Theological Debate in Gal 2:11-21 65

2.6 The Limits of Table- Fellowship in the Judaism of the Late Second Temple Period 66

2.7 Theology of Ethics in Paul 67

2.7.1 The Background of Pauline Ethics 68

2.7.2 The Theological Structure of Paul's Ethic 70

2.7.2.1 Indicative and Imperative 70

2.7.3 The Three Basic Motifs of Pauline Ethic 72

2.7.3.1 Theological 72

2.7.3.2 Eschatological 73

2.7.3.3 Christological 73

2.7.4 Central Place of Morality 74

2.7.5 Social Ethic as well as Community Ethic 75

Summary 76

Chapter 3: Pauline Christological and Missiological Framework and His Gentiles Mission 79
Introduction 79
3.1 The Origins of Paul's Christology 80
3.1.1 Judaism 80
3.1.2 Hellenism 80
3.2 Paul's Conversion/ Call and Early Christian Tradition 81
3.3 The Narrative Framework of Paul's Christology 82
3.4 The Divinity and Humanity of Jesus Christ in Paul's Christology 82
3.4.1 Christ's Divinity 82
3.4.1.1 "Christ… the Wisdom of God" 82
3.4.1.2 "Messiah… God Blessed" (Rom 9:5) 83
3.4.1.3 "Who being in the Form of God…" 83
3.4.1.4 Christ and the Spirit 85
3.4.2 The Humanity of the Christ 85
3.4.2.1 Christ as Son 85
3.4.2.2 Last Adam 86
3.5 The Significance of the Resurrection 88
3.6 Christ as the Image of God 89
3.7 Paul's Christology in His Thought World 90
3.7.1 Eschatology 90
3.7.2 The Meaning of Eschatology and Jewish Understanding 90
3.7.3 Eschatology in Pauline Corpus 92
3.7.3.1 Παρουσία 93
3.7.3.2 Ἀποκάλυψις (Revelation, Declaration) 93
3.7.3.3 Ἐπιφάνεια (Appearance) 94
3.7.3.4 Eschatologia (End of Times) 94
3.7.3.5 Ἡμέρα (Day) 94
3.7.4 Paul on Resurrection 95
3.7.5 Paul on Judgment of God 96
3.7.6 Paul on the Wrath of God 96
3.7.7 Albert Schweitzer Views on Eschatology 96
3.7.8 Eschatology as a Vital Foundation 100

3.7.8.1 The Eschatological Tautness that leads towards the Concept of "Already but Not Yet" 101
3.7.9 Eschatological Contribution: Albert Schweitzer Views and Understanding 102
3.8 Soteriology 103
3.8.1 Colossians 1:15-20 104
3.8.2 Phil 2:6-11 105
3.9 Paul's Mission to Jews and Non-Jews: A Theological Debate 107
3.10 Law and its Significance at Antioch 110
3.11 The New Perspective on Paul 112
3.11.1 E.P. Sanders 112
3.11.1.1 Covenantal Nomism 113
3.11.1.2 Transfer Terminology 114
3.11.1.3 Soteriology 114
3.11.2 James D.G. Dunn 116
3.11.2.1 Justification 116
3.11.2.2 Work of the Law 117
3.11.3 Nicholas Thomas Wright (N. T. Wright) 119
3.11.3.1 The Gospel 119
3.11.3.2 Doctrine of Justification 120
3.12 Some Critiques of NPP 121
Summary 123

Chapter 4: Reinterpreting Paul's Confrontation with Peter in the Light of Redefinition of Christian Identity in a Pluralistic Context 127
Introduction 127
4.1 Religious Pluralism in India 128
4.2 Caste System and Its Impact on Society 128
4.3 Hindu Nationalism and Its Ideology 129
4.4 Eating Habits in India and Socio-Cultural Dynamism 130
4.4.1 *Sangat* in Sikhism: The Common Gathering for eating and fellowship 131

4.4.2 Eating Habits in Hinduism 132
4.5 Christian Identity in India 133
4.5.1 Religious Persecution and Conversion 133
4.6 Paul's Corporate Christological and Soteriological Framework and Model of Pauline Christianity among Converts in North India 134
4.6.1 Paul's Corporate Christology 134
4.6.2 Paul's Corporate Soteriology 140
4.6.2.1 The Meaning of the Term 140
4.6.2.2 Damascus as the Turning Point 141
4.6.2.3 The Role of Triune God 141
4.6.2.4 Symbolism of Soteriology in Pauline writings 142
4.7 Salvation and Grace 147
4.8 Who will be Saved? 148
4.9 The Process of Salvation 148
4.9.1 Salvation in the Past 149
4.9.2 Salvation Now 150
4.9.3 A Future Salvation 150
4.10 Discrimination within the Church and Model of Petrine Christianity 151
4.11 Religious Freedom and Christianity in India 153
4.12 A Socio-Cultural Search for Christian Identity in Pluralistic Context 154
4.13 The Story and Doctrine of Lord's Supper: An Archetype for Christian Identity 155
4.14 Best Example for Christian Identity in India: Paul or Peter 156
4.15 Implications 157
Summary 158

Chapter 5: General Conclusion 161

Bibliography 167

Foreword

Rev. Ashok Kumar's book *Socio-Historical Context of Paul's Confrontation in Galatians and Christian Identity in a Pluralistic Society* is a welcome addition to the field of New Testament. Being an enthusiastic researcher, Rev. Ashok has been able to contribute genuinely and creatively. In this book he mainly discusses the issue of identity and constitutive elements of mission in a religiously pluralistic context. In Galatians, Paul discusses the question of religious identity by taking the then socio-political milieu seriously.

The religious identities of the migrants in the case studies should be seen as an indication to the complex nature of religious identity today. The destructive power of social hierarchy often demolishes the dreams and aspirations of the people on the edges. However, it is the responsibility and task of the genuine religious communities to uphold the dignity and status of human community.

The ministry of publication is very important as part of knowledge activism in India as our context is indeed a challenging one. May God continue to use Rev. Ashok to write more books to strengthen the New Testament scholarship in India.

Rev. Dr. C. I. David Joy
Professor of New Testament
United Theological College, Bangalore

Abstract

This research has several purposes: the first objective is to understand why Paul confronted to Peter at Antioch. Secondly, in the setting of Antioch's scene, how Paul emphatically declares both his independence from the Jerusalem apostles and the fact that, when they did meet, they agreed on the substance of the gospel and divided their areas of work. Thirdly, how eating together and socio-culture, religious issues related to it affect the identity of individual and community both in Galatians and Indian context. Fourthly, to understand Christological and Missiological framework of Paul and to relocate and redefine the Christian identity in pluralistic context based on Paul's Gentile Mission. Finally, to see who serves the best model/example of Christian identity in India, Paul or Peter?

This study proposes to draw significance of eating together that becomes discernible from the texts. As Paul confronts the issue at Antioch, he stresses certain concerns pertaining to social, religious and ethnic identity in Galatians.

The issue at stake in Antioch consisted, quite simply, in the question: were Jewish Messiah-believers allowed to sit and eat at the same table as non- Jewish Messiah-believers? Paul's reconstruction of what happened goes in four stages.

First, the church in Antioch had been used to eating all together irrespective of their ethnic origins. Second, Peter happily joins in the table- fellowship. Third, when certain people came from James, Peter changed his policy. Fourth, Paul calls their act as an act of hypocrisy. The second stage of Paul's argument focuses on Jewish Law and how does it function in the lives of the both Jewish Christians and non-Jewish Christians.

The Christological framework of Pauline thought helps; how cultural-national-ethnicity plays a key role in the formation of Christian Identity. How does each culture have its own representation of Christ? Culture in the contemporary context is no more a closed, static and sold entity. Rather, the engagements and interactions between different cultures have made it highly multiple, fluid and open. Cultural experiences in today's context have two uniquely distinct poles-the inherited pole with the specific ethnic experience that are carried on through heritage and the acquired pole with the experiences received into the overall cultural domain, resulting from the interactions and engagements with 'other culture.' In this particular context, Indian Christians having associations to many different cultures and traditions undoubtedly undergo transculturalism.

All of Paul's confrontations and arguments entreat the church as a community of believers in the Lord Jesus Christ where he focuses on individual liberty. The mutual upbuilding and upholding corporate identity as believers in Christ are main crux of Paul's confrontation with Peter.

Acknowledgment

Reinterpreting Paul's Confrontation with Peter in Galatians 2:11-21 and its significance for a redefinition of Christian Identity in a Pluralistic Context has been a very special project, brought inspiration in my life. I am deeply grateful to my God, my family members, especially to my parents (Sh. Chota Ram Rana and Smt. Sumitra Devi) for their contribution in my life.

I express sincere thanks:

- To the United Theological College, Bangalore to silhouette my theological discernment.
- To the Senate of Serampore University.
- To my respected guide Rev. Dr. J.G. Muthuraj for his luminous inputs on this project.
- To the Biblical department of UTC, Bangalore, especially I thank to Rev. Dr. C. I. David Joy and Rev. Dr. Dexter Maben.
- To the Bangalore Evangelical Lutheran Church, Bangalore and all the leaders especially, to Mr. Puran P. Kujur and for his support and love.
- To Rev. Mustaq A. Malk and Rev. Shivrak K. Mahendra for encouraging me.
- To the Christian World Imprints, especially to Mr. Sudhanshu Kanda.
- Finally, to my wife; Anita Patil Ram Rana, both daughters; Apoorva Ram Rana and Ashank Ram Rana

Introduction

Background of the Research

The tension between Jews and Gentiles is a well-recorded and gravid debate within the field of biblical exegesis today. In Galatians' context why the theology behind Paul's confrontation of Peter and Peter's attitude is understood as a dilemma among the New Testament Theologians? Was the withdrawal from "Eating Together" with Gentiles of Peter was grounded on the appropriate reasons which might be circumcision, Jewish purity requirements or fear of identity? Why Peter was afraid of such extremists in Antioch, when he was prepared to bread with them in Jerusalem, is a problem that cannot be explained without remembering our own psychological "kinks"? Who serves the best example of Christian Identity in pluralistic context; Paul or Peter? It is in this light, this study attempts to exegetically analyze Paul's confrontation of Peter, Peter's attitude and redefine the Christian identity in a pluralistic context.

An Elaboration

One of the biblical passages that directly relates to this special situation, often labelled the "incident of Antioch" in Gal 2.11-21. In this passage Peter (Cephas), an early disciple of the Jesus movement that regularly ate and drank with the Gentiles, is told to draw back and sit in isolation as soon as an orthodox (Jewish) 'fraction of circumcision' (the party of James) arrives from Jerusalem. The struggle lies in the traditional view that this withdrawal represents a conflict between early Christianity (Paul) and Judaism (James) -by many different scholars and distinguished names within the exegetical community commonly held opinion.

Moreover, there are also questions with regard to the situation in Antioch. Clearly, the arrival of Cephas must have occurred prior to Paul's confronting him. Was the one church made up of Gentiles and Jewish Christians? Which of them did Cephas join? Was the act of table fellowship with the Gentile Christians his own personal decision or did it include others? Did the meal include Cephas and the Gentile Christians, or a Gentiles - as well as Jewish-Christian party? Was the meal some kind of demonstrative act or an unplanned incidental event?[1]

We cannot be sure about the purpose of Cephas' visit, but it was probably not out of hostility toward Paul as his participation in the table fellowship shows. We are not sure about the time of visit, either, though some commentators agree that it was not long after the decision on circumcision at the Jerusalem Council.[2] In any case, Paul opposed Cephas to his face (κατά προσόπον), because "he stood condemned" (κατεγνωσμένος ἦν). The verb καταγινώσω is a strong word to use, denoting more than mere ethical or moral wrongdoing, but being "condemned in the sight of God."[3]

Paul's initial counter argument to Peter's action is to point up its inconsistency.[4] What in the world caused Paul to pronounce such judgment on one of the "pillars" of the earliest church? Paul goes on to explain the situation of the church at Antioch. No matter

1 Hans Dieter Betz, *Galatians: A Commentary on Paul's Letter to the Churches in Galatia* (Philadelphia: Fortress Press, 1979), 106.

2 G. Ebeling, *The Truth of the Gospel: An Exposition of Galatians* (trans. David Green; Philadelphia: Fortress Press, 1988), 112.

3 Donald Verseput, "Paul's Gentile Mission and the Jewish Christian Community Study of the Narrative in Galatians 1 and 2" *New Testament Studies* 39 (January, 1993), 36-58.

4 N.T. Wright, *Paul and the Faithfulness of God* (Minneapolis: Fortress Press, 2013), 854-855.

why Cephas came to Antioch he was participating in the "table-fellowship" with Gentiles believers. Paul's use of συνήσθτευ could be interpreted in various ways.

It could refer to "ordinary meals with Gentile believers" or the Lord's Supper or both. The imperfect tense suggests that Cephas ate with Gentiles believers repeatedly and habitually. This "table fellowship" surely was a shocking practice to the Jews considering their tradition (cf. Acts 10:28; 11:2). The practice signifies the actualization of the salvation in Christ who broke down the wall between God and human beings as well as the Jews and the Gentiles. It was an apocalyptic celebration of "the gospel of truth." Breaking up this fellowship is not only the threat to the gospel but actually the denial of it.[5]

In the context of this passage, where Cephas and other Jewish Christians withdrew and separated themselves from eating with the Gentiles Christians when they appeared, these people should be the delegation from James himself.[6] Two imperfect verbs (Ù πέστελλεν and ἀυώριζεν) are inceptive, denoting the gradual beginning of action. Paul's explanation was that he was afraid of "the Jews" (τοÙ ςέκ περιτομής). It is in this light, is there any need of an investigation about the behavior of the two Giants for a redefinition of Christian identity?

The incident of Antioch reminds us that we also face similar situation in our day today's life in which various indifferences are causing and effecting the Christian values and faith. Therefore, such type of debate becomes a stumbling block for the new converts as well as to our neighbors. It is in this context, who serves the best example of Christian identity in a pluralistic context.

---

5 F. F. Bruce, *The Epistle to the Galatians: A Commentary on the Greek Text* (Grand Rapids: William B. Eerdmans Publishing Company, 1982), 126-129.

6 J.B. Lightfoot, *The Epistle of St. Paul to the Galatians* (Grand Rapids: Zondervan, 1965), 112.

Purpose of Research

The main purpose of this research is to study the Paul's confrontation and understand its varied significance in paving a way towards redefinition of Christian identity and religious freedom. Some key aspects will be addressed are: what is eating together and is it necessary to have such type of practice to understand Paul's mission to Gentiles? In what sense the writer bring out this incident in his writing? Is there any possibility to understand συνέσθίω and related terms in relation to redefine Christian identity and religious freedom in a pluralistic context? And how is it possible to bring unity, love, equality and freedom?

Methodology

The exegetical study of the select passage and the entire research will be done from Socio-Political, and liberationist perspective in the context of Conversion, applying insights from liberation hermeneutics. Socio-political method will also be employed to bring clarity to the meaning of the text. A Socio-political method enables the study of the context in which the text was written, probably a world constructed out of the materials of tradition, culture and social conventions available to the author.[7] According to G.R. Osborne hermeneutics and social context play a significant role to uncover or to recreate the social world of the text into conformity with the current needs.[8]

Previous Research

Margaret M. Mitchell argued that Paul and Peter are hypocrites due to failure of their standpoints towards mission to Gentiles in the article entitled "Peter's Hypocrisy" and Paul's: Two "Hypocrites" at the Foundation of Earliest Christianity?" *New Testament studies* 58 (April, 2012): 213. Verseput, Donald analyzes this

---

7 Herman C. Waetjen, *A Reordering of Power: A Socio-Political Reading of Mark's Gospel* (Minneapolis: Fortress Press, 1989), 2-3.

8 G.R. Osborne, 473.

pericope from mission perspective in his article entitled "Paul's Gentile Mission and the Jewish Christian Community Study of the Narrative in Galatians 1 and 2" *New Testament Studies* 39 (January, 1993): 36-58.

There are quite a number studies done on the social setting of Pauline Christianity. The notable one is Gerd Theissen's *"the social setting of Pauline Christianity: essays on Corinth*" in which he extensively deals with social nature of the early Christian community. Recently, John K. Chow in his work, "*patronage and Power: A Study of the Social Networks in Corinth,* extensively deal with the phenomenon of patronage that governed relationships in the Roman world. These two works show how Roman Imperial power influenced the Christian communities.

Stanley J. Samartha, Imtiaz Ahmad, John Hick, Raymond Panikkar, Interreligious dialogue, Michael Barnes, and Gerald H. Anderson talk about pluralism and its significance. However, as far as my reading concern there is no work which directly deals the Antiochen incident recorded in Galatians from the perspective of religious pluralism.

The author will try to evaluate and find the appropriate solution by interpreting Paul's confrontation with Peter based on the socio-political and sociocultural setting of the Galatians context. This attempt will help to understand the theology of Christian identity during Pauline Christianity as well as in our own context.

Scope and Limitations

The study of few related issue will be done from Acts of Apostles. Secondly the author will analyze Paul's understanding based on 1Cor 9:19-23; 11:17-22. Moreover, the focus will be around Galatians.

Chapter 1

Historical and Socio-Cultural Context of Paul's Confrontation in Galatians

Introduction

Paul's letter to the Galatians is one of the fiercest and most polemical writings in the Bible. It begins with a denunciation of those to whom it was written and of unnamed troublemakers (1:6-9). It dismisses another group of Christians as 'false brothers', and accuses Peter of Hypocrisy and deceit.[9] Therefore, the aim of this chapter is to (1) discover the historical account of confrontation in Biblical History; (2) to understand the Galatians' context; (3) to study the religious-political and socio-cultural Issues in Galatians; (4) to bring out the significance of Jerusalem council and Its impact on Galatians Christian community and lastly (5) to know more about Paul as person and Apostle.

9 James D.G. Dunn, *The Theology of Paul's Letter to the Galatians* (Cambridge: Cambridge University Press, 1994), 1.

1.1 Destination of Galatians

Paul addressed in his letter to the "churches in Galatia" (1:2) and rebuked the recipients for being "foolish Galatians" (3:1) some scholars[10] medieval and Reformation commentators argue that the letter was written to churches in or near Ancyra, Pessinus and Tavium, three cities in northern Asia Minor.[11] Those who have this "North Galatia" hypothesis take Acts 16:6 ("the region of Phrygia and Galatia") and Acts 18:23 ("the region of Galatia and Phrygia") as reference to the Paul's missionary trips to "North Galatia" from their perspective "Galatia" in these verses designates the northern region of Asia Minor, not to the Southern Phrygian and Lyconian regions. And also they believe that Paul refers to a particular racial group when he addresses the Galatians.[12]

Other scholars notably W. Ramsay, Bruton, Bruce, Longenecker and Mitchell argue that the "church in Galatia" was planted by Paul as record in Acts 13-14.[13] Those who hold to the "south Galatia" address for the letter take Acts 16:6 and Acts 18:23 as reference to the Paul's return trips to South Galatia. The weight of evidence seems to be in favor to South Galatians location supported by Hemer.[14] It is not surprising that patristic commentators followed by medieval and Reformation commentators assumed that Paul had addressed his letter to

10 J. B. Lightfoot, *Saint Paul's Epistles to the Galatians* (Michigan.: Zondervan, 1957), 18-35.; Hans Dieter, Betz, "Epistles to the Galatians." in *Anchor Bible Dictionary*, 872-75, Edited by D. Freedman. 6 vols. New York: Doubleday, 1992.

11 This tertiary was conquered by a distinct ethnic group of Celtic (Gaulish) descent in third century B.C.

12 Lightfoot, *Saint Paul's Epistles to the Galatians*, 19-21; Dieter, Luhrmann, *Galatians: A Continental Commentary*. Translated by O. C. Dean (Minneapolis: Fortress, 1992), 2.

13 In Acts 13-14- Pisidian, Antioch, Iconium, Lystra and Derbe in South Asia Minor and gentiles from diverse ethnic origins-Phrygians, Pisidians, Lyconians.

14 Colin, Hemer, *The Book of Acts in the Setting of Hellenistic History*. Edited by C. Gemf (Winona Lake, Ind.: Eisenbranus, 1990), 307. In G. Walter Hansen, *Galatians* (Illinois: InterVarsity, 1994), 16.

churches in North Galatia since that was the only Galatia that existed in patristic times.

Thus, with this background we need to understand why Paul addresses them critically and what confrontation means and how the biblical history portrayed it. In this task, the attempt is to deal with the confrontation that occurred at Antioch in Galatians.

1.2 Confrontation

James C. Scott categorizes the practices and forms of confrontation into three groups such as material, status and ideological.[15] Therefore, confrontation can either be overt or covert, onstage or offstage, militant or innocuous, large scale or local level, and also it can either be political and cultural oriented or religious based resistance.

Amit Bhattacharya defines confrontation as "the act or process that induces in the subject an opposition to, refusal to accept or comply with, and the ability to withstand somebody or something."[16] According to Douglas Haynes and Gyan Prakash, confrontation means "those behaviors and cultural practices by subordinate groups that contest hegemonic social formations, that threaten to unravel strategizes of domination; 'consciousness' need not be essential to its constitution."[17]

1.3 Historical Account of Confrontation in Biblical History

The history of Israel is greatly pervaded by several forms of confrontation. Initially, the prophetic movement was one the best examples of confrontation. Prophetic massages contain warning,

---

15 James C. Scott, *Domination and the Arts of Resistance, Hidden Transcripts* (London: Yale University Press, 1990), 198.

16 Amit Bhattcharya, "Unclaimed and Unredeemed: Gender, Marginality and Kamal Das' Poetics of Resistance," *Artha Journal of Social Sciences* 10/2 (July-December 2011): 16.

17 Douglas Haynes and Gyan Prakash, "Introduction: The Entanglement of Power and Resistance," in *Contesting Power: Resistance and Everyday Social Relations in South Asia,* edited by Douglas Haynes and Gyan Prakash (London/Delhi: Oxford University Press, 1991), 3.

prophecy, divine council, oracles and call for repentance. Secondly, confrontation to the domination of the Seleucid dynasty and their associates in the second century BCE in particular is quite palpable. Thirdly, we find another example of confrontation in the Letter of Aristeas. Fourthly, we find various accounts of confrontation in the Gospels and in the Pauline writings.

1.3.1 Prophetic Movement as an Example of Confrontation

Prophets were heard to deliver Yahweh's own utterance to Israel, and as intercessors they were effective in speaking Israel's urgent petitions to Yahweh.[18] Prophets were indeed specific, un-credentialed individuals and who were understood as having a noticeably intimate connection with Yahweh, which made them effective channels of communication between Yahweh and Israel.[19] Prophets are, as John Barton observes, "non-establishment figures who will not be silenced"[20] and responded to crisis or some time evoked crisis," says Walter Brueggemann.[21]

Specifically, In the pre-exilic period the prophets are regularly in encounter with kings, who are perceived as being entrusted with great responsibilities for Yahweh and who have characteristically failed in their implementation.[22] Elijah (1kgs 18:1, 17; 21:17) and Micach (1kgs 22:8) are juxtaposed to Ahab in the ninth century. Isaiah in the eighth century deals in turn with Ahaz (Isa 7:3-17) and Hezekiah (Isa 37:1-7). Amos has his "close encounter" with Amaziah, priest of Jeroboam (Amos 7:10-17) and Jeremiah deals with Zedekiah (Jeremiah 37-38).[23] The prophets deal with

18 Walter Brueggemann, *Theology of the Old Testament: Testimony, Dispute, Advocacy* (Minneapolis: Fortress Press, 1997), 622-623.

19 Joseph Blenkinsopp, *Sage, Priest, Prophet: Religious and Intellectual Leadership in Ancient Israel* (Louisville: Westminster/John Knox Press, 1995), 115-165.

20 John Barton, *Oracles of God: Perceptions of Ancient Prophecy in Israel after the Exile* (London: Darton, Longman and Todd, 1986), 112.

21 Brueggemann, *Theology of the Old Testament…*, 624.

22 Brueggemann, *Theology of the Old Testament…*, 625.

23 Brueggemann, *Theology of the Old Testament…*, 625.

dominant modes of power and dominant definitions of reality. The prophets spoke in outrageous and extreme figures because they intend to disrupt the "safe" construal of realities which were sponsored and advocated by dominant elites.[24]

The prophets have confronted in biblical history in four ways: (1) they were the medium of acute awareness of distress (Amos 5:2; Zeph 1:15-16; Jer 4:31); (2) prophets have presented various images of new possibility (Ezek 37:11-12; Zech 9:9; Micah 2 :1-5; 5:2,4-5); (3) they were Yahweh's own utterance and practitioners of rhetoric and (4) they were the medium of divine council (1Kgs 22:19-23; Jer 23:18, 21-22).[25] Nathaniel Ndiokwere says that "with the books of Esther and Judith, and the books of Maccabees, Jewish thought developed the capacity of confrontation of the poor and down-trodden people in the face of imperialism."[26]

Nathaniel Ndiokwere further states that "with the book of Daniel, it forges into an apocalyptic hope and eschatology of victory over every type of imperialism. The Apocalyptic of John appears from outside to be a point of meeting of all the forces of spiritual confrontation, gradually accumulated in biblical prophetism."[27] The prophetic movement clearly stands out for: criticism of autocracy, despotic action and the condemnation of religious syncretism.[28] Therefore, the prophetic movement is an example of confrontation for marginalized against the dominants norms and structures.

1.3.2 Confrontation During Maccabean Revolt

The Maccabean revolt (a religious and political confrontation of Jews) is remembered one of the great confrontations in the Jewish history. According to John Holder, three 'fundamental theological

24 Brueggemann, *Theology of the Old Testament...*, 625.

25 Brueggemann, *Theology of the Old Testament...*, 625-630.

26 Nathaniel Ndiokwere, *Prophecy and Revolution* (London: SPCK, 1981), 139.

27 Ndiokwere, *Prophecy and Revolution...*, 139-140.

28 Ndiokwere, *Prophecy and Revolution...*, 139-140.

features'[29] from the revolt have emerged: firstly, the emergence of apocalyptic literature that claimed to reveal what would happen in the future, the secret plans of God; for example: the book of Daniel an apocalyptic idea was a hope for an ideal communitarian identity. Secondly, God's ideal community is the kingdom, a source of peace, prosperity and security for the righteous. Thirdly, Messiah and his righteous rule as a symbol of hope that these conditions will one day be transformed into conditions of justice, righteousness and true nationhood.[30]

Maccabean revolt was a confrontation for their identity against the dominant structures of the Hellenism and imperial powers.[31] The cult was the basis of interpretation, means of survival in the foreign land and by which the exiles could be guided back to their home land.[32] John Holder states that Jewish hope was kept alive and the concept of 'conditions now' and 'conditions to come' was influence of the Maccabean revolt.[33]

The ancient strivings of the Maccabees for freedom and Jewish survival provide a source of historical inspiration for modern struggles for Jewish independence. Their disenchantment with Hanukah as a political holiday has two sources. It may have grown out of the political conflicts between the early Pharisees, the predecessors of the rabbis, and the Hasmonean kings who generally favored the Pharisees' rivals and opposing party, the Sadducees. Their disenchantment may also have its sources in the Rabbinic understanding of history, in which God is the prime actor. In addition, in light of the failures of the later revolts against Rome, for which the Maccabean struggle served as a model, it was necessary for them to deflate messianic expectations and pretensions by removing radically the human element in the event.

---

29 John Holder, *The Intertestamental Period* (London: SPCK, 1994), 52-71.

30 Arvid S. Kapelrud, *Israel: From the Earliest Time to the Birth of Christ* (Oxford: Basil Blackwell, 1966), 121-125.

31 Kapelrud, *Israel: From the Earliest Time to the Birth of Christ*, 122-125.

32 Holder, *The Intertestamental Period*, 48-51.

33 Holder, *The Intertestamental Period*, 51.

In this light, the Maccabees succeeded not because of their valour but only because they were agents of God's spirit. Furthermore, neither of our two major historical sources for the Maccabean revolt, First and Second Maccabees, exerted much influence on the rabbinic tradition.[34] Maccabees is a Greek abridgement of a now lost history of the Maccabees written in Greek by Jason of Cyrene. Although it may have been revered by the Greek-speaking Jews of Alexandria, Jews did not consider it to be Scriptural - not only was it a late composition, but it was also written in Greek.[35]

On the other hand, I Maccabees which has come down to us in Greek translation, was originally composed in Hebrew and survived in Hebrew until at least the fifth century C.E. In spite of this, it too was not considered Scriptural. Rabbinic literature does not refer to it and Josephus was willing to amend its account, something he did not do to material he considered Scriptural. I Maccabees did not enter the Hebrew canon not only because it was a late composition. Its pro Hasmonean bias and its tacit rejection of resurrection made it unacceptable to the Pharisaic Sages who were generally anti Hasmonean and who held a strong belief in the world-to come.[36]

The rabbis' rejection of the political aspects of Hanukah has its roots in the Maccabean struggle itself. The revolt marks the rejection of radical Hellenism by the broad spectrum of the Jews united under the charismatic leadership of the priest Mattathias and his five sons. It is difficult to identify all the various groups and interests united under the Maccabees. Since their Jewish opponents seem to have been members of the urban, Jerusalem aristocracy, one can assume that the Maccabees found support among other groups. These might have included members of the rural priesthood and aristocracy-people of the same class and

34 Judah Nadich, *Jewish Legends of the Second Commonwealth* (Philadelphia: The Jewish Publication Society of America, 1983), 67-68.

35 Jonathan Goldstein, *I Maccabees* (Garden City, New York: Doubleday and Company, Inc., 1976), 36.

36 Goldstein, *I Maccabees*, 26.

status as the Maccabees themselves (1 Macc. 2:17) - the urban middle and lower classes, the lower priesthood and religious loyalists from many different levels of society.[37]

When their hope proved unfounded, the Hasidim again joined with the Maccabees and the history of the following twenty years is the history of the struggle of the Maccabees, first led by Jonathan and later by his brother Simon, to achieve Judean independence.

Hanukah is the celebration of the success of the Maccabean revolt. In a way it could be described as the independence day of the second Jewish commonwealth. Hanukah does not, however, mark the end of the revolt. The Jews achieved full independence only in 140 B.C.E., long after the liberation of the Temple. Hanukah rather celebrates an event early in the revolt: the liberation, cleansing and rededication of the temple.

Hanukah celebrates the first major victory of the Maccabees, the victory in which the religious autonomy of the Jews was re-established. Hanukah was not the only holiday decreed by the Maccabees in celebration of their successes. What is significant is that Hanukah is the only one to have survived as a Jewish festival. Hanukah was the only "new" holiday that transcended its national-political foundation and the factional discord that plagued the Jews in the post-Maccabean times.

The Jews in Judea were an ethnos, an autonomous people governed by their own authorities who were led by the High Priest. The High Priest himself was appointed by the reigning king from the High Priestly family to rule the Jews. It is this reform which sparked the Jewish revolt. In its broadest sense, it changed the political status of the Jews and Judea. The reform threatened the autonomy of the Jews for it included an attempt to replace their traditional constitution, the Torah, with a new political-religious system based on the principles of Hellenistic civilization.[38]

Scholars continue to debate about the primary causes which prompted the reform. There are two opposing models. One is that

---

37 Goldstein, *I Maccabees*, 26.

38 Victor Tcherikover, *Hellenistic Civilization and the Yews,* translated by S. Applebaum (New York: Atheneum, 1975), 175-185.

the Hellenistic reform was an internal Jewish development that was supported by Antiochus IV. The other is that the Hellenistic reform was imposed on the Jews from the outside by Antiochus IV. There can be very little doubt that by the second century B.C.E. the Jews were familiar and conversant in the then world culture which we now call Hellenism. Hellenism is the postclassical flourishing of Greek culture that followed the sudden expansion of Greek political influence through the conquests of Alexander the Great and his successors.

The Maccabean revolt does not mark the rejection of Hellenism and the Hellenistic world. The Jews did not retreat into the hill country of Judea after the revolt. They rather asserted their national spirit through economic and political expansion. Quite to the contrary, the Jews became, as a result of the revolt, more involved in the world than they had been previously.

What the Maccabean revolt rejected was the radical reshaping of the political and social structure of the Jewish people from an ethnos rule by traditional law Jerusalem. To accomplish this, they enrolled the leading men of Jerusalem as citizens of the new entity, Antioch at Jerusalem, they established Greek municipal institutions such as a gymnasium, and they changed the worship in the Temple to conform to the practices of worship in other Greek cities. As the honorary founder of the city, Antiochus IV was honored in the traditional manner by a special cult. Many Jews knew Greek and were familiar with Greek popular philosophy, particularly Stoicism.

The extent of Hellenism in Jewish circles is well known and has recently been explored again by Martin Hengel, a German historian, in his book Judaism and Hellenism. Hengel stresses the extent of Hellenism in Judea as well as in the diaspora.[39] In both, the Maccabean revolt is seen as a struggle for political and religious independence. On the one hand, Hengel correctly points

39 Martin Hengel, *Judaism and Hellenism*, translated by John Bowen (Philadelphia: Fortress Press, 1974), 183-185.

out the Jewish commitment to the Torah formed the ideological basis of the revolt.[40]

We can only hope that the Jewish struggles for survival and independence in modern times will provide future generations of Jews with the same strength and wealth of tradition that grew out of the efforts of the Maccabean period.[41]

1.3.3 The Letter of Aristeas

The object of the writer of 'the Letter of Aristeas' is to demonstrate the supremacy of the Jewish People-the Jewish Priesthood, the Jewish law, the Jewish philosophy and the Jewish literatures.[42] Aristeas endeavors to show the real significance of the law with regard to unclean food, and he is especially ingenious in his interpretation of the 'cloven hoof' and chewing the cud.'[43] John R. Bartlett suggests that "the author's purpose is apologetic rather than simply historical."[44] Some scholars argue that the author is defending Judaism, its antiquity and philosophical respectability, to Gentile world.[45] Moreover, the most cogent reason for supporting that the addressees were in the first place Jews and the letter's aim is to justify the translation into Greek of Jewish Law.[46]

Secondly, the author is apparently supporting the authority of the Greek translation of the Jewish Law made in Alexandria[47] which was the equal of the original Hebrews version,[48] the letter of Aristeas is Jewish propaganda directed against the Leontopolis temple, priesthood and scriptures. The author seems to defend

40 Hengel, *Judaism and Hellenism*, 186.

41 Tcherikover, 175-183.

42 R.H. Charles, ed., *the Apocrypha and Pseudepigrapha of the Old Testament in English* (Oxford: The Clarendon Press, 1964), 85.

43 Charles, ed., *The Apocrypha and Pseudepigrapha…*, 88.

44 John R. Bartlett, *Jews in the Hellenistic World* (London: Cambridge University Press, 1985), 11-12.

45 Bartlett, *Jews in the Hellenistic World…*, 12.

46 Bartlett, *Jews in the Hellenistic World…*, 12.

47 Bartlett, *Jews in the Hellenistic World…*, 12-13.

48 Bartlett, *Jews in the Hellenistic World…*, 13.

a form of Judaism that was thoroughly at home in Hellenistic Alexandria.[49] Thirdly, the author quite deliberately seems to reduce the cultural gap between the Jews and non-Jews.[50] R.J.H. Shutt opines in volume of the Old Testament Pseudepiygrapha edited by James H. Charlesworth that there is some affinity between Jews and Greek but not necessarily an identity.[51] However, he further says that Jewish community lived among a predominantly Gentile population. There were obvious differences in culture and religion but Judaism and Hellenism largely succeeded in living side by side there in comparative harmony.[52]

Thus, in the person of Aristeas, he was urging Ptolemy to release Jewish captives.[53] Finally, demonstrating God is one; an benefactor of the human race, providing them health and food and everything else in due season and Jewish Christian belief as compatible with Gentiles are the main features of the Letter of Aristeas.[54] Therefore, it presents an example of Jewish confrontation for their cultural identity and how did they live harmonious life among the Gentiles in Alexandria.

1.3.4 Confrontation in the Gospels and Paul's Letters

In the context of eating together, Michael S. Northcott states that Christ challenges and confronts the power relations implicit in imperial meals (Lk 14:11).[55] But for Christ, the moral economy of food also involves a change and confrontation to the poor diet and disease to which the landless and poor were consigned by the

49 Bartlett, *Jews in the Hellenistic World...*, 12-13.

50 Bartlett, *Jews in the Hellenistic World...*, 12-13.

51 James H. Charlesworth, ed., *The Old Testament Pseudepigrapha,* Vol. 2 (New York: 1985), 7-8.

52 Charlesworth, ed., *The Old Testament Pseudepigrapha...*, 8.

53 Bartlett, *Jews in the Hellenistic World...*, 14.

54 Bartlett, *Jews in the Hellenistic World...*, 14-16.

55 David Grumett and Rachel Muers, eds., *Eating and Believing: Interdisciplinary Perspectives on Vegetarianism and Theology* (London: T&T Clark, 2008), 237.

imperial economy and thus the politics of eating confronts and offends religious and imperial authority.[56]

He further says that the meals in which Christ regularly participates in the gospels and which take center stage in the gospel of Luke, represents paradigmatic act of confrontation to the Roman imperial economy.[57] Christ's choice to eat with those whom debt, poverty, prejudice, illness or association with the Romans, had placed outside the sphere of the righteous, causes embarrassment to his own disciples and outrage among the Pharisees and other rabbis.[58] In a similar way, Dennis Smith argues that the Eucharist as practices by Christians in the first century was the regularization of the many meals that Jesus shared with tax collectors, sinners, Pharisees and disciples throughout his ministry.[59]

Paul confronted at the church of Corinth where the rich enjoyed good food while poor ate ordinary food. By calling church as the "Body of Christ" he means that the body is to discern the significance of the way of Christ, which was the way of common sharing in which all are having equal participation for everything.[60] Moreover, Paul confronted against the Jewish dietary laws that do not give much freedom to Non-Jews. Having this background, let us see the Galatians' context.

1.4 Social Sciences and Galatians' Context

Most social scientific investigations of Paul's epistle to the churches of Galatia explore themes of specific pericope. For instance, John H. Elliott, Jerome H. Neyrey, and Susan Eastman insist that "fear of the Evil Eye" was a pervasive phenomenon in the ancient world-a socio-anthropological reality most commentators of the epistle

56 Grumett, *Eating and Believing...*, 237.

57 Grumett, *Eating and Believing...*, 237.

58 Grumett, *Eating and Believing...*, 237.

59 Dennis E. Smith, *From Symposium to Eucharist: The Banquet in the Early Christian World* (Minneapolis: Fortress Press, 2003), 2.

60 Grumett, *Eating and Believing...*, 239-240.

overlook.[61] Others like Philip F. Esler, James D. G. Dunn, Paula Fredricksen, John Barclay, and Mark D. Nanos investigate Judean and non-Judean social interactions.[62] These scholars agree on the salient nature of socio-anthropological dimensions of nascent Christianity in Galatia. Although Esler's sociological commentary remains the most comprehensive study,[63] major social scientific readings of Galatians have since appeared.[64]

A crucial aspect of these studies has to do with the making of Galatian communities. Community formation, identity, and freedom are categories central to earliest Christians as they are

---

61 John H. Elliott, "Paul, Galatians, and the Evil Eye," *Cross Current in Theology and Mission* 17 (August 1990): 262–271, argues that the word βασκαίνω connotes the idea of "envy" and "to injure the Evil Eye" instead of "bewitched" as most English translations would have it. Like his contemporaries, Paul believed in malevolent forces ascribed to deities, animals, and people with disabilities such as himself. The implication is that Paul was countering the same charges of malevolence of which his opponents have accused him. Jerome H. Neyrey, "Bewitched in Galatia: Paul and Cultural Anthropology," *CBQ* 50 (1988): 72–100. Like John Elliott, Neyrey laments the fact that socio-anthropological aspects of Paul's *Sitzim Leben* are ignored at the expense of theology. Susan Eastman, "The Evil Eye and the Curse of the Law: Galatians 3.1 Revisited," *JSNT* 83 (2001): 69–87. She argues that Paul's converts learned that the curses recorded by the Deuteronomist are tantamount to the casting of the "evil eye" (Deut 28:53–57).

62 Nanos, ed., *Galatians Debate*, 199–318. Philip F. Esler, "Making and Breaking an Agreement Mediterranean Style: A New Reading of Galatians 2:1–14," *BibInt*3 (1995): 285–314, is expanded in his *Galatians* (NTR; ed. John Court; New York: Routledge, 1998) and in Nanos, *Galatians Debate*, 261–81. See also, Nanos, *Irony*; John M. G. Barclay, "'Neither Jew nor Greek': Multiculturalism and the New Perspective on Paul," in *Ethnicity and the Bible* (ed. Mark G. Brett; New York: E. J. Brill Publishers, 1996), 197–214; Philip F. Esler, "Group Boundaries and Intergroup Conflict in Galatians: A New Reading of Galatians 5:13-6:10," in *Ethnicity and the Bible* (ed. Mark G. Brett; New York: E. J. Brill Publishers, 1996), 215-240.

63 Phillip F. Esler, *Galatians* (London/New York: Routledge, 1998), 93-140.

64 Susan Elliott, *Cutting Too Close for Comfort: Paul's Letter to the Galatians in its Anatolian Cultic Context* (New York: T & T Clark International, 2003), 248. And Atsuhiro Asano, *Community-Identity Construction in Galatians: Exegetical, Social-Anthropological and Socio-Historical Studies* (Sheffield: Sheffield Academic Press, 2005), 285.

to modern Christians. A significant sociological model is one that "investigates biblical texts as meaningful configurations of language intended to communicate between composer and audiences."[65] The epistle communicates a poignant message designed to reaffirm and shape the identity of his Galatian converts in Christ,[66] and could not distanced itself from Judaism.[67] Religious reform is often the result of internal discords which could lead to sectarianism. Christianity arose from Judaism and due to ensuing discords over the nature of grace, laws governing circumcision and foods, along with notions of human and cosmic transformation.[68]

This way of delving into the epistle to the churches of Galatia is what Esler calls "biblical inter-culturalism, a hermeneutics derived from social rather than philosophical sources,"[69] and what

65 John H. Elliott, *What is Social-Scientific Criticism?* (Minneapolis, MN: Fortress Press, 1993), 7. Whether Social Scientific Criticism is a "*sub-discipline of exegesis*" or not is debated (Elliott, *What is*, 1). Idem, "Social-Scientific Criticism of the New Testament: More on Methods and Models," *Semeia* 35 (1986): 1; idem, *A Home for the Homeless: A Sociological Exegesis of 1 Peter, Its Situation and Strategy* (Philadelphia, PA: Fortress Press, 1981). Contra John Elliott, Bruce J. Malina is convinced that the social scientific method is a self-contained discipline much like other disciplines that contribute to the historical critical method [Bruce Malina, "Reading Theory Perspective: Reading Luke-Acts," in *The Social World of Luke-Acts: Models for Interpretation* (ed. Jerome Neyrey; Peabody, MA: Hendrickson, 1991), 1–23]. I argue that Paul's message to the churches of Galatia is intricately linked to their socio-religious experiences and convictions.

66 Esler, *Galatians*, 1–2; Idem, *Community and Gospel in Luke-Acts: The Social and Political Motivations of Lucan Theology* (Cambridge: Cambridge University Press, 1978), 1–23. Esler offers crucial insights into how communication is used to shape group identities in the first-century Mediterranean world.

67 Gerd Theissen, *Social Reality and the Early Christians: Theology, Ethics and the World of the New Testament* (trans. Margaret Kohl; Minneapolis, MN: Fortress Press, 1992), 202–227. (Esler, *Community and Gospel*, 16–21; Watson, *Paul, Judaism*, 19–20).

68 Theissen, *Social Reality and the Early Christians…*, 202-227.

69 Esler, *Galatians*, 4. Idem, *New Testament Theology: Communion and Community* (Minneapolis, MN: Fortress Press, 2005), 38–66.

Bruce J. Malina and John J. Pilch refer to as a dialogue between "high context" and "low context" cultures.[70]

Both authors argue that "high context culture" (such as first-century Mediterranean context) have a keen knowledge of elements and concepts embedded in their conversations missing in those of a "low level culture" (just as in modern and postmodern worlds dimensions of communication are missing leaving gaps to be filled). So, when Paul speaks of Jews and Gentiles, he does not have to say that he meant "Judeans" and "Everyone Else." They knew that in their Mediterranean context, one is either Greek (civilized) or barbarian (including Judeans).This is the argument Esler makes in his *Galatians*, 3–5. To bring the meaning of these communications to bear on our own context, an investigation into socio-anthropological.[71]

For instance, Paul reaffirms the identity of his addressees insisting that it is διά πίστεως Ίησοῦ Χριστῷ "through faith in Jesus Christ" that they were liberated from being compelled to *Judaize* (Gal 2:14, 16), from ethnic, class, and gender domination (Gal 3:28). The soteriological significance of their new faith and identity has profound implications ushered in by καινήκτίσις, "a

70 Bruce J. Malina and John J. Pilch, *Social-Science Commentary on the Letters of Paul* (Minneapolis, MN; Fortress Press, 2006), 5–9.

71 Bruce J. Malina and John J. Pilch, *Social-Science Commentary on the Letters of Paul* (Minneapolis, MN; Fortress Press, 2006), 5–9. [Elliott, *What is Social-Scientific Criticism?* Malina, "Reading Theory," 1–23]. Crucial to this discipline is its salient function in safeguarding against the "twin pitfalls of ethnocentrism and anachronism" [Bruce J. Malina, "Social Sciences and Biblical Interpretation," *The Bible and Liberation: Political and Social Hermeneutics* (rev. ed.; ed. Norman K. Gottwald; New York: Orbis Books, 1989), 12; idem, *New Testament World: Insights from Cultural Anthropology* (3rd rev. ed.; Louisville, KY: Westminster John Knox Press, 2001), 7]. The conviction that "*all humans are entirely the same, . . . all humans are* entirely different . . ., and somewhat the same and somewhat different" should remind the reader of the intricacies involved in bringing ancient texts to bear on contemporary concerns (Malina, *New Testament World*, 8).

new creation,"[72] (Gal 6:15; 2Cor 5:17) in which the enslaving στοιχεῖα τοῦκόσμου, "elements of world,"[73] are abolished.

Everett Stonequist insists that a marginal or liminal person is one whose identity is divided by virtue of living between two different and conflicting worlds.[74] This analysis offers invaluable insight into the complex nature of how humans negotiate their identities between worlds. With this social background, let us sees some of the key features of Galatians.

1.5 Religious-Political and Socio-Cultural Issues in Galatians

1.5.1 Conversion

Conversion is a beginning and could be understood as crossing the boundary or an external act of religious change. But it should not

72 *LSJM*, "κτίσις," 1003; BDAG, "κτίσις," 572–3. The term κτίσις denotes the act of creation (Rom 1:20), that which is created (Rom 1:25; 8:19–22, 9; Heb 4:13; 9:11; Col 1:15, 23; 2 Cor 5:17; Gal 6:15; 2 Peter 3:4; Mark 10:6; 13:19), authoritative "founding actions" and governance, colonization (in Greek literature). In the Hebrew Bible, κτίζω is "almost exclusively reserved" to God's creative act (אָרָ·בָ). See also H. H. Esser, "κτίσις," *NIDNTT* 1:378–87. Of the sixty six occurrences in the LXX, sixteen translate אָרָ·בָ (see W. Foerster, "κτίζω, κτίσις, κτίσμα, κτίστης," *TDNT* 3.1000–1035). The LXX however translates κτίζειν variably: אָרָ·בָ; (to create, he created or creates), ק,נָה,עָמַ־ד,וּכּ,יָצַ־ר,יָסַ־ד, and שָׁ כַּ־ן. [See Hatch and Redpath, *CS*, 795].

73 H. Balz, "κόσμος," *EDNT* 2:309. This term belongs to a broad semantic field and is variably used by classical, Hebrew Bible and New Testament writers. In this work, the term κόσμος will be discussed in conjunction with καινὴκτίσις. Against J. Baumgarten who understands Paul's εἴτιςἐν Χριστῷ, καινὴκτίσις "if anyone is in Christ he/she is a new creation," only in anthropological terms (J. Baumgarten, "καινός," *EDNT* 2:229), this work argues that the expression καινὴκτίσις (2 Cor 5:17; Gal 6:15) has anthropological and cosmic implications because Paul understands τάστοιχεῖα τοῦκόσμου to have affected human life as well as the cosmic realm (Gal 4:1–3). The Christ-event on the cross (Gal 3:10, 13) not only transforms but also moves those in Christ into a new theonomy. In Josephus, καιναὶκτίσεις conveys the idea of "founding" or "constructing" of "new settlements" (Josephus, *Ant*, 1.52; 18.373; *J.W.* 4.533; 6.269, 408, 437, 441; see also κτίσις, κτίσμα, κτίστης in Rengstorf, *CCFJ*, 1.1087).

74 Everett Stonequist, "The Problem of the Marginal Man," *AJS* 33 (1935): 3.

be the only time in the Christians' lives when change and renewal take place. For this reason it is a mistake for many Christian's theologians and students to spend much time whether Paul's experience was conversion or call rather looking ahead Paul's contribution to the Gentiles Christian community. It is noticed that despite the great success the gospel enjoys among Gentiles in acts, it is repeatedly rejected by Jews.

1.5.2 Eating Together and Converts' Fellowship

The first century Antioch was a center for different philosophies, cults and religions.[75] It was a meeting point for various civilization and culture. Jewish community at Antioch had attracted great numbers of Gentiles who were even ready to conform to Jewish practices to make possible regular social intercourse including at least guest friendship and table-fellowship.[76] The religious interaction and toleration of Antioch must have provided more space and freedom for conversion. However, since this group of converts was consisted of both Jews and Gentiles, the city's population had to fine a name for them in order to distinguish them from rest of the devotees of the pagan religious in the city. Moreover, Antioch with its mixed nature became the focal point of disputes over circumcision and the observance of the law.[77]

Tissa Balasuriya and N.T. Wright observe that "the table fellowship of Christ was the means to redemption for sinners, so Christian eating becomes an acted parable of a moral economy which recalls the idealized moral economy of the Mosaic covenant and which was enacted in the community of the kingdom that Christ in his earthly life established around him. In the kingdom, and thus at the Eucharist, the poor no longer have their land expropriated from them for the benefits of the tables of the wealthy, but instead are welcomed to the Messianic banquet alongside the rich, where

75 Longenecker, *WBC*: Galatians, 70.

76 James D.G. Dunn, "The Incident at Antioch: Gal 2:11-18," *JSNT* 18 (June, 1983): 27.

77 Dunn, "The Incident at Antioch..., 27-28.

they find not only place, but a voice in the gathering around the breaking of the bread."[78]

1.5.3 James' Impact on Peter's Withdrawal

Robert Jewett proposes that both the Antioch incident and Galatians controversy should be understood against the historical background of a rising Zealot movement and Jewish nationalism in Palestine that advocated radical separation from Gentiles in the late 40s until the Jewish war in A.D. 66.[79] In addition, Jewett's thesis implies that when certain men came from James, Peter began to draw back and separate from Gentile believers because of the fear of Zealot minded Jews and James' Impact.[80]

Certainly, it is evident that peter was under the James' influence. Eating together at the table fellowship would have been a usual practice for Jews and Gentiles. Most probably the meal included the agape meal of which the celebration of the Lord Supper was an integral part.[81]

1.5.4 Jewish Purity Requirement

The incident at Antioch was the precise nature of the meal which was the main concern based on the Jewish purity requirement which was expected from all followers.[82] In addition to this, John P. Meier further suggests that next to circumcision the most important boundary markers that kept Jews an identifiable group was the law of the ritual purity, especially the law pertaining to

78 Tissa Balasuriya, *The Eucharist and Human Liberation* (London: SCM, 1977), 18-20; N.T. Wright, *Jesus and the Victory of God* (Minneapolis: Fortress Press, 1996), 95-97.

79 Robert Jewett, "The Agitators and the Galatians Congregation," *NTS* 17/2 (January, 1971): 205.

80 Jewett, "The Agitators..., 205.

81 George, *NAC*: Galatians, 173.

82 For example, 1 Macc 1: 62-63; Dan 1:8-16; Tobit 10-13 are few example of such requirement. John P. Meier, "Biblical Reflection: The Conflict at Antioch (Gal 2:11-14)," *Mid-Stream* 35/4 (October, 1996): 472.

clean and unclean food.[83] Paul's fundamental discussion of the Gentile Eucharist in 1 Corinthians is preceded by an extensive discussion on the issue of meat eating and the problem of meat offered to idols and as N.T Wright suggest, "this discussion is not epiphenomenal to his account of the Eucharist. On the contrary, the economy of eating was problematic in Corinth because it was a pagan economy in which meat butchered at pagan temples."[84]

Thereby, the issue was the failure of the Christian Jews, including Peter to maintain separation from Gentiles. Paul makes his point clear that he opposed Peter to his face. Whatever political pressures may have been exerted on Peter, Paul could not tolerate his action. By withdrawing himself from the table fellowship Peter was acting not only against his consciousness but also against his recent past practices in Antioch.

1.6 The Concept of Ecclesiology in Paul

The ecclesiology of Paul is confined within the gathering of the Christian community. The early Christians communities keep increasing wherever Paul lives in and he calls the assembly of his community as ἐκκλησία, church. Many small groups are found in various region and these groups in coming together fall under "the whole church" and are considered as the local community. As a result, Paul addresses the Christians as "the church" in his epistles and uses certain metaphors in order to relate it to their fat and for the spiritual growth and to maintain certain discipline in the church. Therefore, this discussion provides us how Paul defines the ἐκκλησία and the metaphors used for the enhancement of the local community.

---

83 Meier, "Biblical Reflection..., 472.

84 N.T. Wright, 'One God, One Lord, One People: Incarnational Christology for a Church in a Pagan Environment,' *Ex Auditu* 7 (1991), 45-58.

1.6.1 Greaco-Roman World

In the early century colonization of the Mediterranean by the Rome, spread the Greek culture throughout the entire territory.[85] Many gods were recognized in the Greaco-Roman world.[86] The believers struggled to keep their identity in midst of the complexities of Greaco-Roman world. But Paul's communities not only stand for their group but also mirrored re-created humanity as conversion takes place (Gal 3:28; 2Cor 5:17).[87] In such a context two major groups were existed in which the people correlate themselves: "*Politeia*, the public life of the city or nation state to which people belonged; and *Oikonomia,* the household order into which they were born or to which they were attached."[88]

Greek citizens during the fifth century played a vital role in the city where Paul lived and in the house headed by him. But there were some weaker section of the people who could not be part of either of these two communities, however sought place in the smaller community.[89] The Gentile converts find less space to participate as normal members of the Greaco-Roman household (*Oikonomia* 1Cor 10:21).[90] Moreover, some thoughtful societal members looked beyond the city of cosmopolitan order where everyone would be included and developed equally. But some assumed that it as abstract and exclusive in the one hand, or unrealistic on the other. However, number of associations emerged according to the interest of the member in the polis for the social elites particularly in Greek centers.[91]

---

85 Robert Banks, *Paul's Idea of Community* (Massachusetts: Hendrickson Publishers, Inc, 1994), 6.

86 Margaret Y. Macdonald, *The Pauline Churches: A Socio-Historical Study of Institutionalization in the Pauline and Deutero-Pauline Writings* (Cambridge: Cambridge University Press, 1998), 170.

87 Macdonald, *The Pauline Churches...*, 32-39.

88 Banks, *Paul's Idea of Community…*, 6.

89 Banks, *Paul's Idea of Community…*, 7.

90 E.P. Sanders, *Paul, the Law and the Jewish People* (Philadelphia: Fortress Press, 1983), 176.

91 Banks, *Paul's Idea of Community…*, 7.

According to Gerd Theissan the church leaders attain the utmost social status among members.[92] But in the late Hellenistic period a wider group emerged from the socially disadvantaged members of the society that brings people regardless of race, class, and background.[93]

1.6.2 ἐκκλησία

During the Paul's missionary Journey, the Christian community throughout the Mediterranean region increased rapidly.[94] Church takes the vital place in Paul's thought yet he seldom talks about the doctrine of church in his writings. Eschatology and Christology are the element of Paul's ecclesiology and their interconnection establishes the character and function of the church. Paul takes the term ἐκκλησία from believers' community at Antioch.[95]

His expression "the whole church" refers to the local church which also describes the gathering of the Christians at same place as an assembly for "the Lord's Supper" in Corinth (1Cor 11:20). The Corinthian church consist of diverse groups and so the word "gathering" is best describe as "church" (1Cor 11-14).[96] The term ἐκκλησία appears approximately 66 times in Pauline writings. Embracing gospel becomes entering into community. It is from 5th century that the word ἐκκλησία referred to "the regular assembly of citizens in a city to decide matters affecting their welfare."[97]

In other words Paul refers this term to a local church or a concrete assembly of Christians.[98] This concept established during

---

92 Macdonald, *The Pauline Churches...*, 40.

93 Banks, *Paul's Idea of Community...*, 8.

94 Banks, *Paul's Idea of Community...*, 28.

95 J. Christian Baker, *The Triumph of God: The Essence of Paul's Thought,* translated by Loren T. Stuckenbruck (Minneapolis: Augsburg Fortress, 1990), 99-100.

96 Vincent Branick, *the House Church in the Writings of Paul* (Delaware: Michael Glazier Wilmington, 1989), 23-27.

97 Banks, *Paul's Idea of Community...*, 26-27.

98 George A. Maloney, *The Cosmic Christ: From Paul to Teilhard* (New York: Sheed and Ward, 1968), 60.

Paul's 3rd missionary journey Ephesus (Act 19:21-24) when the silversmiths were scared of the impact of Paul's preaching against idol worship and criticizing against his ministry. And so such matters are discussed and decided in έκκλησία (Acts19:39). Then the meaning of έκκλησία is non-religious term. For the Jewish people έκκλησία is used to translate the Hebrew word for the "assembly" of the people of Israel before God and hardly renders to *synagogue*.

The term 'assemblies' vary in character religiously, politically and spontaneous assemblies. "έκκλησία simply means an assembly or gathering of people in a quite ordinary sense" and so in Greek the term implies to meetings which are secular by nature.[99]

Therefore, then Paul conceptualized the corporate identity of those converted in the Gentiles mission within the term 'church.'[100] And as believers in Christ "the whole church is that *koinonia* which belongs to Christ and in which he is present." For this reason in the act of redemption the church is the body of Christ that reveals the new creation.[101]

1.6.3 Purpose of έκκλησία

1.6.3.1 Paul's Usage

From the early period the term 'church' is a common word in Christian use before the time of Paul which means that the early communities gathering is differed from Jewish assemblies and Hellenistic cults.[102] And so, it is suggested that Paul's usage was derived from Israel's self-identity. έκκλησία appears 100 times in LXX and in Hebrew the word basically appears as *qahal*, "*assembly*" and phrases as *qahal Yahweh or qahal Israel*. LXX translate this phrase assembly of the Lord and also *synagogue* for

99 Banks, *Paul's Idea of Community*..., 26-28.

100 James D.G. Dunn, *The Theology of Paul the Apostle* (Grand Rapids: William B. Eerdmans Publishing Company, 1998), 537.

101 Eric H. Wahlstrom, *The New Life in Christ* (Illinois: Muhlenberg Press, 1950), 225.

102 Banks, *Paul's Idea of Community*..., 29.

qahal. "The church of God" serves Paul's purpose much better.[103] However, *synagogue* which is for Jewish community is never implied to Christian gathering in the New Testament. Paul first used the term while greeting Thessalonica's Christian (1 Thess 1:1) in same manner with Greek and Jewish circle, yet maintains distinction from other assembly of the city.

The closing of the letter conceives Paul's notion of Thessalonian Christians as a 'regularly gathering community' (5:26-27) and in 2 Thess 1:1, the added words "in God the Father," "έκκλησία" and phrase "in the Lord Jesus Christ" deprive the political outlook.

The phrase "churches of God" in Judea refers to Christians gatherings in plural form. This description implies to "an actual gathering of People" or the group that assembles as "a regularly constituted meeting." Besides, the other literary form also gives evident towards the reference to έκκλησία for instance in Gal 1:2; Rom 16:4, 16 give the plural reference to έκκλησία. Such plural references as the churches in Galatia (Gal 1:2; 1Cor 16:1), "churches of Asia" (1Cor 16:19), "churches in Macedonia" (2Cor 8:1) and the churches of Judaea (Gal 1:22) differ the notion of national church from that of Paul's universal church and is simply is known by provinces than addressing generally as "the churches of the saints" or "the churches of the Gentiles" (1Cor 14:33; Rom 16:4)." On the other hand, the opening lines of the Thessalonians' and Galatians' letter remind the existence of church through Christ from God. And so, έκκλησία refers to not only the gathering concept but also a 'divinely created affair.'[104]

1.6.3.2 Church as Gathering

In Paul's greetings to his readers in the later part of the letter of 1 Corinthians writes "together with the church in the house" where the term οἶκος could be the quarters inhabited by Priscilla and Aquila or the household under them unlike Acts. The former suggests the home of Priscilla and Aquila as meeting place for the

103 Dunn, *The Theology of Paul the Apostle*..., 537-538.

104 Banks, *Paul's Idea of Community*..., 29-31.

Christians in Ephesus while the letter refers to the entire household that comprised the gathering. But the οἶκος sometimes refers to slaves. In Corinth small groups of believers exist and assemble together in the meeting of the whole church whereas in Rome the whole church never assembled in one place unlike Corinth. And so, Paul addresses as "to all God's beloved in Rome, who are called to be saints" (Rom 1:7). In Paul's early letter έκκλησία is rendered to "actual gathering of Christians" or "to Christians in a local area conceived as regularly assembling community." Unlike 3rd century building for Christians gathering were not there but assemble in a room which holds about 30 people.[105]

1.6.4 Metaphor of έκκλησία

Paul often uses metaphors in his thought on community emphasizing at the importance of images he uses:

1.6.4.1 Building

Paul uses the metaphor of building in his writings number of times representing Christian community. An ordinary building and the temple are viewed frequently. Paul considers himself as the master builder to the growth of the community. As temple, Paul emphasizes "its relationship with God through the Spirit and, as a consequence of this, its holiness and the wholehearted service it should render to God."[106]

In the former writings the whole building characterizes the community with the view on the local community whereas in the later writings, the foundation of the building represents Christ himself. This metaphor can also be related to the individual believer or community being portrayed not simply as "stones" in God's building but as "the temple of the Holy Father" (1Cor 6:19). From the household sphere, church is compared with "dough" and the offending member with "leaven."[107]

---

105 Banks, *Paul's Idea of Community...*, 31-35.

106 Banks, *Paul's Idea of Community...*, 47-48.

107 Banks, *Paul's Idea of Community...*, 47-48.

1.6.4.2 Temple of God

Paul sometimes refers "the temple of God" to the Jerusalem temple, but in his letter to the Corinthians, he means the believers as God's temple and the believers body as the temple of the Holy Spirit (1Cor 3:16-17, 19; 2Cor 6:16). In other words Paul implies the temple "constituted by the immediate indwelling of God in individual and people, rather than mediatly through a temple as such (2Cor 6:16) and of such a direct indwelling that it made redundant any continuing (or for Gentile converts, new) royalty to the Jerusalem temple."[108] In this regard, Philo also states the body as "a sacred dwelling place or shine for the reasonable soul." Through this understanding Paul's concept of "the temple of God" can be either understood as in accessing to God's presence no human made temple is required.[109]

1.6.4.3 *Soma*: Body of Christ

Even if the church unity is a gift of God's justifying grace (Rom 5:17-21; 2 Cor 5:14), yet it is attacked always but external and internal forces like quarreling, factions, immorality, church division etc (1Cor 5:1; 1:13). In such phrase Paul relates a Hellenistic-Roman metaphor of the body and its members to the church for positive outlook.[110]

This metaphor as "a unified yet many-membered organism in which each member has its function and the whole could not remain alive without each is far from exhausting Paul's idea."[111] The body refers to the body of Christ given in Christ himself and so he never urges the believers to become the church or the body of Christ, rather he relates the metaphors to communicate the fact of communal participation of the members in the body of Christ.

---

108 Dunn, *The Theology of Paul the Apostle…*, 545-546.

109 Dunn, *The Theology of Paul the Apostle…*, 554.

110 Baker, *The Triumph of God: The Essènce of Paul's Thought*, translated by Loren T. Stuckenbruck…, 100-102.

111 Gunter Bornkamm, *Paul,* translated by D.M.G. Stalker (New York: Harper & Row, Publishers, 1969), 194.

Therefore, the body metaphor elucidates the notion of the mutual participation of the members in Christ and interdependence in the life of the church. Paul's another motif is derived from the Jewish notion of Corporate personality" holding the elements such as: "the one for all" that elucidate 'the death of Christ as the act of God's grace for his people' (Rom 5:12-29; 1Cor 15:22), the "once for all" that states that eschatological-historical event of the death and resurrection of Christ (Rom 5:15-19) and "the one in all" (Rom 5:12-29; 1Cor 15:22). Hence, the unity of the church and the mutual interdependence of its members are seen in *soma* as Christocentric while έκκλησία is theocentric. On the other hand, soma emphasizes the incorporation of all believers in Christ while έκκλησία views to a local community.[112]

The 'one body in Christ' (Rom 12:5) does not refer to the earthly community although it is of the earth and is found in "the one who gave his body to die on the cross and is present on the church." As a result, there is no distinction between Jews and Gentiles, slaves and free persons (1 Cor 12:13, Gal 3:28).[113] It is the church that carries the person and work of Christ and so church is the true body of Christ.[114]

1.6.4.3.1 An Ecclesial Christology

The church is developed by expressing Christ more in individual' faith. Therefore, Paul makes a distinction between Christ and the believers in the metaphor soma as the head and body of Christ and his ecclesiology is distinct in the concept of Christ's church as the body of Christ.[115]

1.6.4.3.1.1 You are Christ's Body

The church is envisioned as the Christian community, either local or universal, mainly by the faith linkage and observation of

112 Baker, *The Triumph of God: The Essence of Paul's Thought*, translated by Loren T. Stuckenbruck…, 100.

113 Maloney, *The Cosmic Christ*…, 70.

114 Maloney, *The Cosmic Christ*…, 59-60.

115 Maloney, *The Cosmic Christ*…, 59-60.

sacrament, baptism and Eucharist.[116] Baptism is assumed as 'the rite of initiation into the community of faith' and expresses the mystical union with Christ (Gal 3:37). In other words 'the baptized person now belongs to Christ' while Eucharist advocates mystical entity (1Cor 10:16).[117] Paul sees church with the 'resurrected Body-person,' Jesus Christ (Eph 1:20-23). His concept on church as the body of Christ was less developed in major writings like Romans (12:4-5) and 1 Corinthians (12:12-27; 6:12-20; 10:17). But in his epistles to the Colossians and Ephesians the doctrine of the believers as the body of Christ is well set up where Christ is the head (Eph 1:22, 23; 5:23, 30; 4:15, 16; Col 1:18, 24; 2: 19).

In this perspective of sacrament (1Cor 12:13; 10:17) the metaphor of church cannot be simply compared with the earthly community yet is of the earth. It reflects on the glorified body of Christ and believers unite with it through baptism and Eucharist. In this regard Benoit expresses this union "under the form of a physical sacramental union of the body of the Christian with the individual body of Christ" and states "without a doubt this 'physical' reality is of a very special type, completely new which is that of the eschatological era begun-while the old era still continues."[118]

Using this metaphor Paul expresses the absolute communion between Christ and Church. The body also conveys the inner unity. And so, in using this metaphor Paul reminds the Corinthians to maintain unity of the church in the context of pride for spiritual gift, quarrelling and jealousy.[119]

1.6.4.3.1.2 Christ, the Head of the Body-Church

The assumption of the relationship of the head to the body in Colossians and Ephesians pictures the relationship between Christ and community where Christ is depicted not only the

116 Maloney, *The Cosmic Christ...*, 60.

117 Jouette M. Bassler, *Navigating Paul: An Introduction to Key Theological Concepts* (Louisville: Westminster John Knox Press, 2007), 41-42.

118 Maloney, *The Cosmic Christ...*, 60-62.

119 Wahlstrom, *The New Life in Christ...*, 224-225.

head of the church but also the one who holds supreme authority (Col 2:10; Eph 1: 21-23).[120] Paul assumed the notion of the head as the director of the whole body (1Cor 12:12-27). Col 2:10 and Eph 1:22-23 portray Christ as the head of the church having the ultimate authority over the world. Paul's ideology further elucidate the head of a body as 'the principle of life, the mover, the nourisher and sustainer of life' (Eph 4:16). Plato presumes the head as 'seat of the nous, reason,' while Hippocrates and Galen, Greek physicians, embrace the notion that 'the head contained the nervous center that directed all the other members.'[121] This relationship emphasizes the immorality of the union.[122]

1.6.4.3.2 Building up the Body of Christ

This theme is distinctly stated by Paul in Ephesians 4:10-16 as Christ filling all the members with his grace. Therefore, Paul elucidates the hierarchical divisions in the body-church in vv 11-13 as the different responsibilities mentioned are the organized significant service rendered for the building up of the church.

> The gifts he gave were that some would be apostles, some prophets, some evangelists, some pastor and teachers, to equip the saints for the work of ministry, for building up the body of Christ, until all of us come to the unity of the faith and of the knowledge of the son of God maturity, to the mature of the full stature of Christ (Eph 4:11-13).[123]

Paul stresses on the importance of the individual member responsibility in connection with the Head for the building of the body of Christ.[124] Thus, each member has his/her own role to play in contributing 'for the harmonious development of the whole' and

120 Macdonald, *The Pauline Churches: A Socio-Historical Study of Institutionalization in the Pauline and Deutero-Pauline Writings*..., 154.

121 Maloney, *The Cosmic Christ*..., 63-64.

122 Macdonald, *The Pauline Churches: A Socio-Historical Study of Institutionalization in the Pauline and Deutero-Pauline Writings*..., 155.

123 Maloney, *The Cosmic Christ*..., 64-66.

124 Maloney, *The Cosmic Christ*..., 66.

to stand together both in good and bad times.[125] Paul's continues urge of "building up the ἐκκλησία" determines the right use of the spiritual gifts (1Cor 14:4, 5, 12, 19-20).[126]

1.7 Jerusalem Council and Its Impact on Galatians Christian Community

The apostolic council was called because some Judean Christians were teaching Gentile Christians in Antioch that they had to be circumcised or else they could not be saved (Act 15:1). However, Luke's readers already knew that uncircumcised people had been given the Holy Spirit and had been baptized (10:44-48). God had called Gentiles to repentance and salvation (11:18), but a formal policy about circumcision had not yet been made.

Many Gentiles had come into the church because of the work of Paul and Barnabas (Acts 13-14, especially 14:27), and it became evident that Gentiles would become a substantial part of the church. It became necessary to clarify some theological and practical details of Gentile membership in the church. Some Pharisees had also become believers (15:5).[127] The council was called to determine how both Pharisees and Gentiles could be part of the same community of believers. For the Jerusalem leaders and those standing with them, this was a matter of great practical concern and they tried to take measures to keep Gentile Christians from needlessly offending Jewish sensibilities, but they were not prepared to make Gentiles Jews (so the decision and decrees of the later Jerusalem Council of Acts 15:1–29).

The "false brothers" referred to in Gal 2:4-5 and the Judaizers who invaded the churches of Galatia, however, turned this practical concern into a theological issue, and so tried to impose a Jewish lifestyle on all Gentile converts.

125 Wahlstrom, *The New Life in Christ…*, 225.

126 Branick, *The House Church in the Writings of Paul…*, 28.

127 Wright, 'One God, One Lord, One People: Incarnational…, 45-48.

1.7.1 Arguments for the Identity Between Galatians 2:1-10 and Acts 15

The purpose of this section is to outline and interact with the traditional arguments in favor of equating Galatians 2:1-10 with Acts 15. According to Donald Guthrie[128] this is the traditional view based primarily, though not solely, upon similarities. Lightfoot says that "In support of this view may be urged the positive argument from the striking coincidence of circumstances, and the negative argument from the difficulty of finding an equally probable solution." It appears that Lightfoot having given himself rather ardently to the North Galatia position would not allow the possibility of Galatians 2 referring to anything but Acts 15. It is essential to his thesis concerning the location of the churches in the North. But, indeed, Acts 11 is "an equally probable solution" as history has shown subsequent to Lightfoot's work. Whether Acts 11 is correct is another matter, but it is equally probable in both accounts.[129]

1.7.2 Similarity in People and Issues

In both Galatians 2 and Acts 15 there is a similarity concerning the people who are mentioned. Both refer to Paul and Barnabas, James and Peter. This seems to lend weight to the idea that these two meetings are really one and the same meeting.[130] And the issues at stake seem to be the same. In both cases Paul and Barnabas seem to be contending against strong opposition from a Judaizing sect.[131]And finally, as Lightfoot[132] pointed out, the geography in the two accounts is the same, namely, Jerusalem and Antioch.

---

128 Gutherie, *Introduction*, 474.

129 Lightfoot, op. cit., 123.

130 Toussaint, op. cit. 335, 336. It should be noted that those who hold to the North Galatia theory have no choice, generally speaking, but to identify Galatians 2:1-10 with Acts 15. see, Gutherie, *Introduction,* 474.

131 Acts 15:1, 2 and Gal. 3:1-3.

132 Lightfoot, op. cit.,123.

However, Boice,[133] who himself holds to Acts 15 being the same event as Galatians 2, lists at least three apparent discrepancies in the accounts. First, Acts gives the impression that Paul and Barnabas presented their case publicly, but Galatians seems to involve only a private meeting with the leaders. There is the possibility that both occurred, with the smaller, private conference preceded the larger, public conference.[134] But this appears to diminish the point Paul is making in Galatians 2:2, wherein he claims that he presented the gospel "privately." Toussaint[135] also observes that such a reconstruction of things makes the Jerusalem council, which Luke so strongly emphasizes, little more than a rubber stamp.

The second and third discrepancy Boice mentions include the fact that Galatians says Titus accompanied Paul and Barnabas to Jerusalem, but Acts does not mention him. And, in Galatians Paul claimed to have gone up to Jerusalem due to a revelation, whereas Acts 15 says they went as envoys of the church. However, these two discrepancies may not be substantial in any way. First, just because Luke does not mention Titus, does not mean to say or even imply that he was not with them. And, on the second point, Paul could have gone up to Jerusalem at the request of the Antiochan leaders as well as a revelation from God.[136]

1.7.3 Paul as the Apostle to the Gentiles

This section identifies Paul's Jerusalem visit outlined in Galatians 2:1-10 with one of his visits enumerated by Luke in Acts. There are five[137] such visits of the apostle to Jerusalem as recorded in the book of Acts, but in the final analysis only two appear to fall

133 Boice, op. cit., 418. The following arguments are succinctly laid out by Boice, though He says that Acts 15 should be paired with Galatians 2 due to the striking coincidence of circumstances. He is following Lightfoot for the most part.

134 Ibid., 419.

135 Toussaint, op. cit. 337.

136 Acts 9:29, 30 with 22:17-21.

137 Acts 9:26-30; 11:27-30, 12:25; 15:1-30; 18:22 and 21:15-23:35.

within the province of reasonable candidates as the referent to Galatians 2:1-10. They are Acts 11:27-30; 12:25 and Acts 15.[138]

Another argument in favor of equating Galatians 2 with Acts 15 is the fact that Paul was recognized as the apostle to the Gentiles in Galatians (cf. Gal 2:8). This would not have been possible if Galatians 2 refers to Acts 11 because there simply would not have been enough time for those in Jerusalem to have recognized this about Paul.[139] Longenecker[140] has sufficiently dealt with Stein's work by demonstrating that it depends too heavily on the book of Acts ignoring Paul's own idea of himself and his calling. It is plain that he received his call to preach to the Gentiles at his conversion as he emphatically states in Galatians 1:15, 16.

1.7.4 A Literary Argument

Another argument in favor of Galatians 2 referring to Acts 15 is literary in nature, having to do with Luke's presentation of the leadership relationship between Paul and Barnabas. Luke says in Acts 11 that "Barnabas and Paul" went down to Antioch, but later in Acts 15 he reverses the order of their names, apparently indicating that Paul was now in command of the team. According to Stein,[141] the fact that Paul is the leader in Acts 15 and appears as such in Galatians 2:1-10 indicates that these meetings should be thought of as the same. But, this appears to ignore the fact that it appears as such in Galatians *because Paul is writing of his experience* in the light of those who are trying to undercut his gospel and discredit him.[142]

---

138 Toussaint, op. cit., 334.

139 Robert Stein, "The Relationship of Galatians 2:1-10 and Acts 15:1-35: Two Neglected Arguments," *Journal of the Evangelical Theological Society* 17 (Fall 1974): 242. He says that at the time of the famine visit Paul had not even gone on his missionary journeys nor had much success in Troas so far as we can tell.

140 Longenecker, op. cit., 81.

141 Ibid., 242.

142 Paul here is not talking about Barnabas per se, but is instead fighting for the freedom of the churches he has planted.

1.7.5 Galatians and Romans

Lightfoot[143] contended that the content of Galatians is very similar to that of Romans, which literary connection he thought, presupposes a similar time frame in which both were written. Since it is a well-accepted fact that Paul wrote Romans during the winter preceding his last visit to Jerusalem (ca. 57 A.D.),[144] it is most likely then, according to Lightfoot that Galatians was written then as well. The natural inference from this is that Galatians 2:1-10 would then refer to the Jerusalem Council of Acts 15.[145]

1.7.6 Εσπούδασα in Galatians 2:10

Burton, in his commentary on Galatians says "that the visit to Jerusalem recorded in 2:1-10 was for the purpose of the relieving the poor of Jerusalem is excluded by the aorist tense of έ σπού δασα"[146] Therefore, Burton[147] says that the famine must have been a while before this Jerusalem visit, since Paul responded to Peter's plea by claiming that it was the very thing he *struggled* (past tense referring in Burton's mind to the famine visit) to do. But this argument is really not that substantial and can be dealt with by seeing that Peter's admonition to Paul came at the end of the visit and thus he was exhorting Paul to continue to remember (μνημονεύ ωμεν (i.e. durative sense) the poor as he had done on this particular occasion. To this Paul simply responded by saying that it was the very thing he had (always) sought (έ σπού δασα) to do.[148]

143 Lightfoot, 48-49.

144 F. F. Bruce, *Galatian Problems* 4: 254.

145 Toussaint, 336.

146 Burton, 115.

147 Stein, *Two Neglected Arguments,* 240. Stein also discusses the similarities such as geography, the issues (i.e. circumcision); the relation between Romans and Galatians, etc.

148 Robert G. Hoerber, 484.

1.7.7 Two Objections

There are two objections that must be dealt with if one accepts Acts 15 as the visit Paul is discussing in Galatians 2:1-10. First, why then does Paul not mention the decree of the council? According to Longenecker[149] this would have served the coup de grace to the conflict in Galatia. Indeed, Boice refers to it as the most serious problem in this scenario. First, he says that the decrees were addressed to Christians in Antioch and Syria and Cilicia, not to Gentiles all over the Roman world. Second, according to Boice, Paul may have very well at a later time, considered the decree concerning restrictions for conscience sake a dangerous concession, likely to be misunderstood. Third, Boice says that if Paul quoted the decree, he would have played right into the hands of those who accused him of getting his gospel from those in Jerusalem.[150]

The second objection raised against equating Acts 15 with Galatians 2:1-10 concerns the reading of Galatians 1:18-2:10. If this theory stands, Paul has omitted one of his visits to Jerusalem, namely, the famine visit, since 1:18-20 undoubtedly refers to his conversion experience (Acts 9:26-30). The normal reading of πάλιν would indicate that the visit in 2:1-10 is the next visit after the conversion visit (Acts 9), i.e. the famine visit. And it has been suggested by many commentators that a failure on Paul's behalf to mention the famine visit may leave his integrity open to suspicion-something his opponents would have made much of.

1.8 Arguments for the Identity Between Galatians 2:1-10 and Acts 11:27-30 and 12:25

The purpose of this section is to surface and evaluate certain arguments that favor the famine visit of Acts 11:27-30 and 12:25 (hereafter simply referred to as Acts 11) as that to which Paul refers in Galatians 2.

---

149 Longenecker, op. cit. 79.

150 Boice, op. cit. 419.

1.8.1 Paul and the Incident with Peter

It is difficult to imagine that the decree preceded the events of Peter's separation from the Gentiles and Paul's rebuking him. Surely Peter, even though he possessed a vacillating spirit, would not have done such a thing after the Jerusalem church, that is, those who caused it the first time (Gal. 2:12), had settled the issue. Indeed, if the confrontation between Paul and Peter occurred after the decree, then it is difficult to imagine that Paul would record such a thing. In such a case he has been further separated from the apostles at Jerusalem. However, the agreement among those at the Council makes such an interpretation tenuous.[151]

One also needs to consider the idea that it is difficult to imagine that the Judaizers could have accomplished so much, as the letter to the Galatians indicates, if Galatians 2:1-10 refers to the Council. The churches so led astray by the Judaizers would have been quite a bit less willing to go along with the heretics if they had knowledge of the decree.[152]

1.8.2 Paul's Work in Syria and Cilicia

In Galatians 1:21 Paul says that he visited Syria and Cilicia. This occurred after his first visit (1:18) and before his second visit to Jerusalem (2:1). This most likely refers to the fact that Paul concentrated his missionary work in Tarsus and Antioch (after Barnabas 'retrieved' him from Tarsus) without going to any other centers. If this is true then, he did not evangelize in Galatia until after his second visit to Jerusalem and therefore, Galatians 2:1-10 must refer to the famine visit with evangelization of Galatia (Acts 13, 14) sometime later.

1.8.3 Two Objections

The first objection concerns the chronological problem inherent in saying that Galatians 2 is equivalent to the famine visit. Most are

151 Longenecker, 80.

152 Bruce, *Galatian Problems,* 4: 252.

in agreement that the famine visit took place around A.D. 46.[153] If one adds up the years Paul mentions in Galatians 1:18 and 2:1, one has 17 years. This places Paul's conversion around A.D. 30, which obviously does not even allow enough time for the growth of the church mentioned in Acts 2-8. This has been solved in at least three[154] ways by various writers: 1) both the three years and the fourteen years refer to the date of Paul's conversion; 2) Paul is using a method of counting years that counts parts of years as full years and 3) to push back the crucifixion to 30 A.D. from 33 A.D. and then to date Paul's conversion about 32 A.D.[155]

The second objection involves the 'former' visit referred to by Paul in Galatians 4:13. Those who hold to the North Galatia theory cite this as a reference to Acts 16:6 and 18:23. But this implies that the phrase τό πρό τερον carries the idea of 'former' only. It may also mean "initially" or "originally."[156] But if the term does mean two visits then it is possible to see them as occurring on his return from the first missionary journey as Luke records him passing back through the cities in which he established churches (cf. Acts 14:21). This would fit well with dating the letter before the Jerusalem Council.[157]

When the evidence is taken into account, though the standard interpretation of Galatians 2:1-10 has been to see it referring to Acts 15, it seems best to refer the Galatians' passage to Acts 11 and the famine visit. There is both solid evidence for this view as well as no insurmountable problems.

---

153 Bruce, *Galatian Problems,* 339.

154 Longenecker, 83.

155 Fourteen years back from 46 A.D. would be around 32 or 33. If Christ were crucified in A.D. 30 then there is no real problem in the chronology. Obviously this is not the place to debate the date of the crucifixion, but a date of A.D. 30 is apparently not uncommon among scholars.

156 Walter Bauer, et al. *A Greek-English Lexicon of the New Testament and Other Early Christian Literature,* trans. by William F. Arndt and F. Wilbur Gingrich, 2nd ed. (Chicago: The University of Chicago Press, 1979), 722. They say that from a lexical point of view it is not possible to establish the thesis that Paul wished to differentiate between a later and earlier one visit.

157 Bruce, *Galatian Problems,* 4: 252.

1.9 Paul's Experience: Conversion or Call?

We find six summaries of Paul's experience in the New Testament, three times in Acts (Acts 9:1-19; 22:1-21; and 26:1-23) and three times in Paul's epistles (Gal 1:13-17; 1Cor 15:8-10 and Phil 3:4-11). However, according to Seyoom Kim there are several other references which alludes to Paul's Damascus road experience such as Rom 10:2-4; 1Cor 9:1, 16-17; 2Cor 3:4-4:6; Eph 3:1-13; Col 1:23-29.[158] The three versions of Lucan account are generally in agreement but there are differences and even contradictions in details.

The experience of Paul is significant for Christianity in a number of ways. According to F.F. Bruce it is the Second most important event in Christian history after the Christ event.[159] There are many attempts have been made over the years to discredit the authenticity of Paul's conversion. Epiphanius Ebionites[160] circulated a story about Paul according to which Paul was not really a Jew by birth but was the son of Greek parents. Later when along with his father Paul moved to Jerusalem he fell in love with high priest's daughter. On order to obtain the girl Paul became a Jewish proselyte and underwent circumcision. Unfortunately, Paul could not obtain the girl he became a furious and began to write against circumcision, the Sabbath and the Law. However, the story has no historical basis it still indicates how attempts were made from very early period to explain the radical change Paul underwent.[161]

Renan's view does not seem convincing because it reflects his own biased negation of the supernatural element in the Christian faith. Others like J. Dupont see utter hopelessness of Pharisaic

---

158 Seyoom Kim, *The Origin of Paul's Gospel* (Michigan: William B. Eerdmans Publishing Company, 1981), 3-31.

159 F.F. Bruce, *Paul: Apostle of the Heart Set Free* (Michigan: William B. Eerdmans Publishing Company, 1979), 75.

160 Cited in Richard N. Longnecker, *Galatians: World Biblical Commentary,* Vol. 41 (Dallas: World Books Publisher, 1990), 26.

161 Timothy George, *Galatians: The New American Comminatory,* Vol. 30 (Nashville: Broadman and Holman Publishers, 1994), 31.

legal righteousness as the factor for Paul's conversion.[162] This also a least possibility because Paul's description of himself as a Pharisees, does not allow much room for such type of guilt feeling (Phil 3:4-6). Moreover, the works of scholars like W.G. Kummel has shown that there is nothing to prove that Rom 7:7-25, is an autobiographical document.[163] Similarly the study of Martin Hengel and A.M. Schwemerhas also stressed that there is no room for any psychological preparation in either in Luke's narratives or in Paul's accounts.[164]

Therefore, there is no doubt that Paul's call is an important part of conversion experience, but this does not define the whole experience. Segal puts it in a better way, "from the view point of mission Paul is commissioned (that indicate to a call), but from the view point of religious experience Paul is a convert."[165] Therefore, rather than talking about conversion **or** call it is more appropriate to talk of conversion **and** call.

Summary

Antioch's incident gave birth to a debate that became a conglomeratic phenomenon for the Biblical Scholars. It provides new identical contexts and hermeneutics for scholars who study to know more Jewish and Gentiles' context. Therefore, this chapter explains how biblical literature itself has a notion of confrontation for example; prophetic movement, Maccabean revolt, the letter of Aristeas and the Gospels including Paul's other writings describe how Jewish had confronted for their socio-religious norms and identity. Secondly, how does Paul's conversion, experience and his identity with risen Lord Influence the Antioch incident.

---

162 J.B. Polhill, *New American Commentary: Acts,* Vol. 26 (Nashville: Broadman Press, 1992), 240.

163 Walently Prokulski Jr., "Conversion of St. Paul," *Catholic Biblical Quarterly* 19/4 (October, 1957): 456.

164 Martin Hengel and Anna Maria Schwemer, *Paul between Damascus and Antioch*tr. By John Bowden (London: SCM Press, 1997), 42.

165 A. F. Segal, *Paul the Convert: The Apostolate and the Apostasy of Saul the Pharisee* (London: Yale University Press, 1990), 6.

Therefore, through this analysis it is assumed that Paul's notion on ecclesiology is held among the believers who experience a new being in Christ and their gathering contributes to one such ideology. Also, the metaphor Christ as the head of the body and each believers as the member of that body forms an ideal Church where each member contributes towards the building of the body by his/her own gifts through grace and where the believers' body is considered as the temple of God. Hence, Paul's understanding of the Christian community as ἐκκλησία and emphasizing its in-depth relationship with the significance of certain metaphors embrace the notion of corporate bond between Christ and human and between human kind in building up the 'One body, One Church'.

Chapter 2

Socio-Cultural Approach to Galatians 2 and Other Related Texts

Introduction

In general understanding Galatians is "one of the four 'capital' epistles of Paul."[166] The opening of an epistle gives an observation unlike other letters of Paul it begins on a polemical note. While he is full of frustration and uses all kinds of abusive words. So, there is no expression of honor (eulogy) for these churches. Why is he mentioning so? Because Paul's immediate statement concerning his apostleship, which seems Galatians were given different account about Paul's apostleship or rejected his apostleship.[167] Moreover churches are threatened by heresy (another gospel). By talking about these he is establishing authority and credibility with absolute rhetorical skill.

Therefore, this chapter briefly explores on Gal: 1:1-11 to examine major issues on the source of Paul's apostleship and

166 F. F. Bruce, "Galatians," (*NIGTC*; Michigan: William B. Eerdmans Publishing Company, 1982), 1.

167 Bruce, "Galatians"…1-2.

preaching of contrary gospel through agitators and it helps to understand the background of the incident at Antioch. Secondly, exegetical studies of the text Gal 2:11-21 explores the socio-political context of the church. Thirdly, discusses the issues that emerged or existed in the church of Antioch.

2.1 Paul's Argument and its Context in Gal: 1:1-11

It is very certain that while Paul's apostleship was questioned by the legalizers takes lot of pain to defend and establish his authority. On the other hand, false teachers were proclaiming "different gospel" that was totally in opposition to "Gospel of Grace".The arguments from theses passages are Paul's defending of his apostleship against agitators and Paul's defending the true Gospel.

Before we can understand Galatians we need to know what Paul is fighting against. He has something thoughtful at the bottom of his argument. The force of the language in v.1 expresses and leads reader to heart of the letter. There is no praise unlike other epistle. Paul estimated the honor which the Galatians did him at this first missionary visit."[168]

2.1.1 Paul's defending of his Apostleship against Agitators

V.1 Παῦλος ἀπόστολος οὐκ ἀπ' ἀνθρώπων οὐδὲ δι' ἀνθρώπου ἀλλὰ διὰ 'Ιησοῦ Χριστοῦ καὶ θεοῦ πατρὸς τοῦ ἐγείραντος αὐτὸν ἐκ νεκρῶν,

Παῦλος ἀπόστολος (Nominative absolute), Paul always highlights himself to be Apostles and commissioned by Jesus to preach gospel. This had been seriously challenged by the Galatians legalizers.[169]

It is "ἀπόστολος" is obviously related with the verb "ἀπόστολω" in classical author it is employed both as an adjective and as a

168 Ronald Y. K. Fung, *The Epistle to the Galatians* (Michigan: William B. Eerdmans Publishing Company, 1988), 198.

169 It is quite possible that Paul did not meet the conditions of apostleship like other Apostles. James Monotogomoery, "Galatians," (*EBC*; Michigan: Zondervan, 1976), 424.

noun "ἀπόστολος" (nominative absolute). So, it is evident from the epistle that Paul's representation of the Gospel declared to be incorrect by the false brothers. Victorinus' earlier statement here suggests "that the authority in question is not that of Paul but that of his gospel, which is basis of the apostle's authority."[170] He has also associated with himself all the brothers who were with him, to the effect that they themselves would be writing to the Galatians, whom he is shaming with the fact that everybody disagrees with them.[171] Here both the apology (defensive response) and Polemic (aggressive explication) are evident.[172]

V. 1ª οὐκ ἀπ' ἀνθρώπων οὐδὲ δι' ἀνθρώπου

The Apostle begins with the emphatic assertion of his authority.[173] Paul strengthens the force of his own precepts and the force of the gospel he is spreading. Obviously, he is intending to correct the Galatians. Lightfoot argues that the "the first clause he distinguishes himself from the false apostles, who did not derive their commission from God at all."[174] Some other scholars points out that "he has in mind about the primitive apostles, in which they were dominant influence, it being from this source that his opponents would told that he ought to have derived his apostleship in order to make it valid."[175] "It is very certain that in no sense his apostleship which is in no sense indirect, dependent, or secondary."[176] This fact is important for the understanding of the whole Galatians.

170 Stephen Cooper Marius Victorinus, *Commentary on Galatians* (New York: Oxford University Press, 2005), 250.

171 Victorinus, *Commentary on Galatians*, 250.

172 Richard N. Longenecker, "Galatians," (*WBC* 41; Dallas, Texas: Word Books, 1998), 5.

173 _______________., The Epistle of St. Paul to Thessalonica, Galatians and Romans, 254.

174 James Monotogomoery, *Galatians*, 425.

175 Burton, *A Critical and Exegetical Commentary*..., 4.

176 Bruce, Galatians, *NIGTC*, 72.

V. 1b οὐδὲ Δι 'ἀνθρώπου "not through the agency of man" (genitive of agency)

The preposition δια' used to indicate "mediation"[177] The word ἀνθρώπου "is abstract, not concrete; it is not necessary to translate by a man."[178] So, it is better to translate "through man" or "through a man."[179]

Zahn interprets οὐδὲ Δι 'ἀνθρώπου as a denial of a charge that he had received his apostleship through a certain unnamed person, most probably Barnabas.[180] "Paul mentions that received it in a way far above this which made human source and human agency completely unnecessary."[181] Most probably Paul's opponent claimed to be standing in the line of the continuity with the Jerusalem apostles and their full and authentic gospel."[182] Manson notes that, "the effect of Paul's emphatic contrast is to say that he does not want the apostolic credentials and the complete Jerusalem version of the Gospel which his opponents in Galatia claimed to have, for his authority and his gospel are alike derived from a different and higher source."[183]

V. 1c ἀλλὰ διὰ 'Ιησοῦ Χριστοῦ καὶ θεοῦ πατρὸςτοῦ ἐγείραν το ςαὐτὸν ἐκ νεκρῶν,

Some scholars find as strange that διὰ "through," is used as the preposition before both 'Ιησοῦ Χριστου and θεοῦ πατρὸς. Burton

177 Bruce, Galatians, NIGTC, 72.

178 __________, The Epistle of St. Paul to Thessalonica, Galatians and Romans, 254.

179 Philip F. Elser, *Galatians* (London: Routeledge, 1998), 70.

180 Ernest De Witt Burton, *A Critical and Exegetical Commentary on the Epistles to the Galatians*, 5.

181 The double genitival use of a;nqrwpojis certainly generic, first in the plural with avpoVto denote source and then in the singular with diato refer to agency. Bruce, "Galatians," *NIGTC*, 35.

182 Ronald Y. K. Fung, The Epistle to the Galatians (Michigan: William B. Eerdmans Publishing Company, 1988), 198.

183 T. W. Manson, *On the Paul and John*, ed., M. Black (London, _______, 1963), 170.

believes, that Paul could have thought of either Jesus Christ or God the Father as an agent."[184] Hence, διὰ Genitive, in addition to its use with reference to spatial and temporal relations, expresses means or instrument, which with a personal object merges into the idea of agency.[185] The idea of agency merging into that of conditioning cause is used with reference to that which, so to speak, stands behind the action and renders it possible."[186]

τοῦ ἐγείραν το ςαὐτὸν ἐκνεκρω– (genitive of separation), The raising of Christ, moreover, was especially relevant to his commissioning."[187] Paul's commission to preach the gospel is directly from God. Its origin lies in him who put the final seal of approval on the very mission of Christ himself.[188]

Why would Paul bring in such big argument such as neither from men nor through agency of man? The agitators brought long list of Paul ineligibility to be an apostle. But for Paul uses heavy words and prepositions to apology (defensive response) and Polemic (aggressive explication) [189] against false brothers.

2.1.2 Argument No: 2 Paul's warning "Not to accept the different Gospel" (VV. 6-10)

Paul is making "the courtroom scene a possible milieu for this section of the letter."[190] In this section, Paul is going to point out Galatians who turned away from the "Gospel of Grace" to "different Gospel."

V. 6 Θαυμάζω ὅτι οὕτως ταχέως μετα τίθεσθε ἀπὸ τοῦ καλέσαντος ὑμᾶς ἐνχάριτι [Χριστοῦ] εἰς ἕτερον εὐαγγέλιον,

---

184 Timothy George, Galatians (*NAC*; USA: Broadman & Holmann, 1994), 81.

185 Monotogomoery, *Galatians*, 6.

186 Ernest De Witt Burton, *A Critical and Exegetical Commentary on the Epistles to the Galatians*, 6.

187 Bruce, "Galatians," *NIGTC*, 74.

188 S. J. Joseph A. Fitzmyer, "The Letter to the Galatians," *NJBC*, 782.

189 Longenecker, "Galatians," *WBC*, 4.

190 Elser, *Galatians*, 56.

T. Y. Mullins argues that in antiquity a letter writer who uses Θαυμάζω "is confronting, even scolding the addressee which is like "ironic confrontation"[191]

2.1.3 The Reasons for Paul Astonishment

Firstly, the passage shows that the apostle is blaming the Galatians for lending listening ear to the trouble – makers false teaching.[192] They abandoned the Gospel which was preached to them. "It is somewhat relative temporal expression."[193] The Galatians had immediately failed from the true faith as soon as they were confronted with the message of the false teachers."[194]

Secondly, the present tense of the verb μετατὶθεσθε," as Burton points out, "indicates clearly that when the apostle wrote, the apostasy of the Galatians was as yet only in process. They were, so to speak, on the point, or more exactly in the very act, of turning"[195] Thirdly, it is argued that Paul had himself in mind, for he was the Christian missioner who first brought the gospel to them.[196]

V. 6 εἰς ἕτερον εὐαγγέλιον, ὃ οὐκ ἔστιν ἄλλο εὐαγγέλιον

"The message which the Galatians' Christians are disposed to accept in place of that which they received from Paul is so different from Paul's message that it constitutes ἕτερον εὐαγγέλιο 'a different "gospel."[197] "Paul is probably implying here that the "different gospel" here is to no other than the false gospel, which is obedience to the law as an added requirement for salvation aside

191 Longenecker, "Galatians," *WBC*, 6.

192 Fung, *The Epistle to the Galatians*, 44.

193 Fung, *The Epistle to the Galatians*, 37.

194 George, *Galatians*, 90.

195 Monotogomoery, *Galatians*, 19.

196 Longenecker, "Galatians," *WBC*, 7.

197 Bruce, "Galatians," *NIGTC*, 81.

from faith in Christ. Thus, the true Gospel, which he is preaching is, "faith in Christ alone, is sufficient for salvation."[198]

2.1.4 The Characterization of the False Teachers' Message

V.7. ὃ οὐκ ἔστιν ἄλλο, εἰμή τινές εἰσινοἱ ταράσσοντες ὑμᾶς καὶ θέλον τεςμεταστρέψαι τὸ εὐαγγέλιον τοῦ Χριστοῦ. "except that some people are confusing you and desiring to pervert the gospel of Christ."

Plural "some people" indicates a plurality of false teachers in Galatia, not a single person. Οἱ ταράσσοντες ὑμᾶς "those confusing you" present tense of the verbs and participles points out the fact that these agitators were still in Galatia when Paul was writing this letter, and that he wrote with the intention of stopping them in the very midst of their activities."[199] The verb ταράσσω "disturb, unsettle, and confuse" mental and spiritual agitation."[200]

2.1.5 Characterization of the Paul's Message

The formula τὸ εὐαγγέλιον τοῦ Χριστου here and elsewhere in Paul must be taken in the same way as in Mark 1:1: the gospel which has Jesus Christ (and God through Christ) as its focus and God (together with Christ) as its source.[201] Whatever you receive evaluate it, so that Christ will not be ashamed of you. What is the main goal of Paul? To simply put, "not to accept other gospel," [202] he draws a clear line between the "Gospel of Grace" and "different gospel" which is absent in other undisputed letters of Paul. Paul's designation of himself as an apostle suggests at the beginning that apostolic authority will be an important feature in his Galatians

---

198 Bruce, "Galatians," *NIGTC*, 81-82.

199 Longenecker, "Galatians," *WBC*, 8.

200 The verb metastrevfw ("change," "alter," "pervert") was also originally a political term, so they want to make revolutionary in churches over against Pauline perspective of the gospel. Bruce, "Galatians," *NIGTC*, 84.

201 The word avna,qema indicates both "indicative" and "imperative". Longenecker, "Galatians," *WBC*, 8.

202 Longenecker, "Galatians," *WBC*, 8-9.

argument. Paul stress is entirely on God as the source of Paul's apostleship.

2.2 Paul's Exposure of Peter's Eating Habits (vv 11-14a)

A number of commentators to postulate that the Antioch episode is not related in its true historical order, but must be seen as having taken place before the meeting narrated in 2:1–10.[203] It is most natural, however, to take the Antioch episode of 2:11–14 as having occurred after the meeting narrated in 2:1–10. And that is how the vast majority of commentators have taken it, whether they see the meeting of 2:1–10 as being the famine visit of Acts 11 or the Jerusalem council of Acts 15.[204]

There is much in 2:11–14 that we are not told about the situation at Antioch, and much of what we are told is mostly by way of allusion. What complex of events led up to Paul's rebuke of Peter? What was the Antioch church like before this incident? When and why did Peter come to Antioch? What issues were at stake-not only from Paul's perspective, but also from Peter's and those Christians of Antioch who joined him in his withdrawal? How did Barnabas view matters? Who really "won" in the dispute? And what was Antioch Christianity like after this episode?[205]

Five stages in the development of the plot at Antioch are identifiable in Paul's account: (1) Peter's practice of eating with Gentile believers *before* a delegation from Jerusalem arrived; (2) Peter's withdrawal from table fellowship with Gentile believers *after* the delegation from Jerusalem arrived; (3) the separation of Jewish believers from Gentile believers as a result of Peter's withdrawal, with "even Barnabas" joining in that separation; (4) Paul's evaluation of the situation, crediting Peter's withdrawal as an act of hypocrisy based on fear and Barnabas's action in

---

203 Augustine,T. Zahn, J. Munck, H. M. Féret, and J. Dupont. Longenecker, "Galatians," *WBC*, 63-64.

204 Longenecker, "Galatians," *WBC*, 64.

205 Longenecker, "Galatians," *WBC*, 64.

following Peter's example as based on irrational emotion; and (5) Paul's open denunciation of Peter.[206]

Paul's discussion on the incident at Antioch is centered on the inconsistency of Peter's eating habits that led to the division within the community. Reasons of Peter's arrival at Antioch are uncertain but Paul's description of the incident shows that when he was at Antioch he at first had no difficulty in enjoying table-fellowship with Gentile Christians. He seems to have freely related with the Gentile believers even to the extent of eating with them (v.12 a.)[207] However, after the arrival of the representative from James, Peter backed out, leaving the gentiles to themselves and entered exclusively in Jewish-Christians communion (v. 12 b). Paul confirms that the arrival of the men from James caused a major breach in the church at Antioch. This behavior created more confusion since even Barnabas along with the rest of the Jewish Christians were all carried away by Peter's action in staying aloof from the gentiles believers (v. 13). Thus Peter's withdrawal from the fellowship with Gentile Christians is immediately questioned.[208]

Cullman asserts that the withdrawal of Peter is in contrast to his convictions.[209] Barrett is of the opinion that what Peter has done is not because of what he believes but out of fear: "It was not conscientious but prudential and is for this reason described by Paul as hypocrisy (συναπήχθη αύτῶν τῇ ὑποκρίσει)."[210]

Manson builds on this explanation and tries to find a genuine cause for Peter's fear. According to him, the news of his free and easy relations with the Gentiles at Antioch had reached Jerusalem and thus proved a stumbling block for those he was seeking to evangelize, besides hampering the mission in which James and

206 Longenecker, "Galatians," *WBC*, 65.

207 B.B. Blue," Food Offered to Idols and Jewish food Laws," in *Dictionary of Paul and His Letters DPL* (Illinois: InterVarsity Press, 1993): 307.

208 Blue," Food Offered to Idols…, 307-308.

209 Oscar Cullmann, *Peter: Disciple, Apostle, Martyr* (Philadelphia: Westminster Press, 1962), 552-553.

210 C.K. Barrett, *Essay on Paul* (Philadelphia: the Westminster John Knox Press, 1962), 95-96.

others were engaged among their Jewish neighbors.[211] However, Bruce holds the view that Peter like Paul (ICor 9:22 ff) must has been trying to be "all things to all men" for the sake of gospel.[212] But this proposition is unlikely because of two reasons: firstly, if Peter was trying to be "all things to all men," he should not have broken off from the Gentile fellowship since he is still at Antioch and not in Jerusalem. Secondly, the text confirms that peter acted in that manner because of fear 2:12. Therefore, as discussed above, it is safe to go with Barrett and others that Peter's action is not because of conviction but out of fear. This brings us to deliberate further by taking some of the sentences, words and phrases on Paul's account of his confrontation with peter's eating habits.[213]

κατά πρόσωπον αύτῷ ἀνέστην, "I opposed him to his face." Longenecker asserts that the idiom κατά πρόσωπον does not by itself necessarily connote hostility, but only direct encounter.[214] Lightfoot,[215] Burton,[216] Bruce[217] and others interpreted it as self-condemnation because of the inconsistency of his own action. However, Longenecker, following Ulrich Wilckens maintains that verb καταγινώσκω implies to "be condemned before God."[218] Therefore, Paul considers Peter's action to be very serious and felt obligatory to confront him forthrightly.

Peter's action according to Paul's understanding is a deviation from the basic Christians faith-God accepted both Jews and Gentiles

---

211 T.W. Manson, *Studies in the Gospels and Epistles* (Manchester: 1962), 180-181.

212 F.F Bruce, *Paul: Apostle of the Heart Set Free* (Grand Rapids, Michigan: William B. Eerdmans Publishing Company, 1977), 177.

213 As above, Bruce, *Paul: Apostle of the Heart Set Free,* 177.

214 The phrase ὅτι κατεγνωσμένος ἦν "because he stood condemned" (v 11b), which highlights Paul's judgment on Peter's behavior is extremely severe. The phrase has been recognized differently in NT scholarship. Longenecker, "Galatians," *WBC*, 72.

215 J.B. Lightfoot, *Saint Paul's Epistle to the Galatians* (London: Macmillan, 1892), 111.

216 E.D. Burton, *Galatians* (Edinburgh: T&T Clark, 1921), 103.

217 Bruce, *Paul...*, 129.

218 Longenecker, "Galatians," *WBC*, 72.

as his people merely on the basis of their faith in Christ and not through their good works or "works of the law."[219] Moreover, the reference of Paul to ά λή θειαν τοῦ εὐαγγελίου, "the truth of the gospel" in v.14 possibly implies the gospel which Christ preached, i.e., the gospel that has no distinction. Therefore, for Paul, Peter's abstaining from eating with the Gentile Christians is nothing but an absolute denial of the fundamental of God's grace due to their conduct that determines a basis for an exclusive rather than an inclusive unity, which is entirely against the self-giving of Christ for others.[220]

But taking περιτομή in this latter sense requires still further clarification, for a definition in terms of standing or character has a number of possibilities. Does it mean (1) Jewish Christians who held a particular partisan view of circumcision, i.e., the Judaizers; (2) Jewish Christians in a nonpartisan sense; (3) non-Christian Jews; or, though far less likely, (4) Gentile Christians enamored by Judaism who had taken on a Jewish perspective and lifestyle, either wholly or in part? The debate has been extensive and often highly convoluted.[221]

Another reason why Cephas' separation from the table of the Gentiles must have been based upon sound reasons is that "the other Jews" followed his example: "also the other Jews committed the same 'hypocrisy' with him, so that even Barnabas was carried away through their 'hypocrisy.'"[222] However, they were not convinced by Paul's reasoning that this happened "through their 'hypocrisy.'"[223]

ἀλλ᾽ ὅ τε εἶ δον ὅ τι οὐ κ ὀ ρθοποδοῦ σιν πρό ς τὴν ἀλήθειαν τοῦ εὐαγγελίου, "but when I saw that they were not acting in line with the truth of the gospel." The strong adversative ἀλλά

219 Gal 3:28.

220 Gal 2:11-14.

221 G. Dix, *Jew and Greek*, 43ff, J. Munck, *Paul and the Salvation of Mankind*, 106-9; W. Schmithals, *Paul and James*, 66-68.

222 G. Dix, *Jew and Greek*, 43ff, J. Munck, *Paul and the Salvation of Mankind*, 106-9; W. Schmithals, *Paul and James*, 66-68.

223 Betz, *Galatians...*, 109.

("but") signals that here in v 14 we have a direct contrast to what is narrated in vv. 12-13.

The question, of course, arises: Why did Paul allow such a process to go on for so long, whatever the length of time, before intervening? Was Paul himself unclear at first as to the implications involved, or perhaps unwilling to voice his opposition openly-or was he unable, for some reason, to speak freely? Or was Paul absent from Antioch during the early part of Cephas's visit, and only knew what was going on when he returned? For, as Burton points out, if the former were true then "Paul himself was involved only less deeply than Peter in the latter's confusion of thought and it is therefore hardly likely that he would have spoken in the words of sharp condemnation of Peter which he employs in v. 11 and in this verse."[224]

Paul points out, was inconsistent with his own habitual practice. Worse than that, however, it was disastrous for the cause of the gospel, for Gentile Christians would have had to become Jews for full acceptance within the church.[225]

Ironically, therefore, by attempting to preserve the integrity of the Jewish Christians as Jews, Cephas destroys the integrity of the Gentile Christians as believers in Christ. Instead of welcoming them as converts to Christianity, he wants to make them into converts to Judaism. This contradicts the principles of the doctrine of Justification by faith, which had been the basis of the faith thus far (2:15-16).[226] The sharpness of Paul's public confrontation of Peter has always stood as a major problem for interpreters of the Antioch episode. But Peter's withdrawal of fellowship turned them into matters of great theological import.[227]

Paul tells us what he said to Peter but he does not tell us how Peter, Barnabas, or the Antioch church reacted to what he said. The omission of such statements in Paul's account has led

---

224 Betz, *Galatians...*, 109.

225 Longenecker, "Galatians," *WBC*, 77.

226 Longenecker, "Galatians," *WBC*, 78.

227 Betz, *Galatians...*, 112.

many to conclude that actually Paul lost and Peter triumphed at Antioch.[228]

The word συνή σθιεν, "he was eating" should be elaborated since the entire problem between Paul and Peter in this text is related to the eating habits between the Jews and Gentiles. Burton argues that the issue involved in the incident at Antioch is simply a matter of Jewish food laws.[229] Similarly, Meeks also asserts that by abandoning the standard Jewish regulations governing eating the "Pauline Christians gave up one of the most effective ways by which the Jewish community had maintained its separate identity in the pagan society."[230]

The imperfect form of συνήσθιεν suggests that he did so repeatedly and almost habitually. Nothing is said whether these meals were ordinary meals, or celebration of Lord's Supper, or both.[231] The point of concern is the Jewish purity requirements which must be observed whatever meals were involved. As a result, cultic separation would have to be observed also during table fellowship with Gentiles Christians.[232]

The present tense of ζῆς ("you are living") implies much more than an act of table fellowship with Gentile Christians. It suggests that the table fellowship was only the external symbol of Cephas' recent change of conduct as a self-contradiction: "how can you compel the Gentiles to live like Jews?"[233]

Apparently, verse 12f. explain that by the time Peter visits Galatia, the church at Antioch had already established a custom of gathering all the believers, irrespective of their identity to enjoy the table-fellowship with another.[234] Then the significant question

228 Longenecker, "Galatians," *WBC*, 79.

229 B. W. Bacon, *JR* 9 (1929) 204–23; H. Koester, *HTR* 58 [1965] 286; J. D. G. Dunn, *Unity*, 254; J. P. Meier, in Brown and Meier, *Antioch and Rome*, 39–40

230 Burton, *Galatians*…, 104.

231 Meeks, *The First Urban*…, 97.

232 Betz, *Galatians*..., 107.

233 Betz, *Galatians*..., 108.

234 Betz, *Galatians*..., 112.

arises; what was the nature of the table-fellowship that Peter enjoyed with the Gentiles and what exactly has it that made him to withdraw when the men of James arrived at Antioch?

By translating the word συνήσθιεν as "taking his meal," Fung argues that there can be no doubt of taking it as connoting "a reference participation in the Lord's Supper."[235] He supports his argument by asserting that the Eucharist and the community love feast were closely linked together ICor 11:20-22, 33f.[236] However, Burton simply says that the verb συνήσθιεν ("he used to eat") implies the ordinary meals with the Gentiles believers.[237] On the other hand Bruce opines that the reference to Peter's eating with the Gentiles could be both social meals as well as Lord's Supper since there is no practical distinction made between the two, and at the same time the "memorial bread and wine were normally taken in the context of a social meal."[238]

Longnecker further observes that imperfect tense of the verb suggests that Peter ate with Gentile believers repeatedly or habitually and not just once.[239] Hence, the assumption of Peter's participation in both meals is evident. But why did Peter have to withdraw from that fellowship? To answer this question, it is necessary to grasp the reason why Jews and Gentiles could not eat together, i.e., what did the food laws mean for a devout Jews? Dunn gives three alternatives of the nature of the table-fellowship practiced by the Christians community at Antioch before the emissaries from James appeared.[240]

Firstly, the table-fellowship which was practiced by the community had relinquished the laws governing the table-

235 Ronal Y. K. Fung, *The Epistle to the Galatians* (Grand Rapids, Michigan: William B. Eerdmans Publishing Company, 1988), 104.

236 Fung, *The Epistle to the Galatians*, 106.

237 Fung, *The Epistle to the Galatians*, 106.

238 Burton, *Galatians…*, 104.

239 Bruce, *Paul…*, 176.

240 Longenecker, "Galatians," *WBC*, 73.

fellowship. This means that they no longer observed the food laws. Dunn Keep this alternative under the doubtful category.[241]

Secondly, the table-fellowship at Antioch possibly had involved a reasonable level of observance of "the dietary laws" including even some of the *Halakic* elaborations concerning tithes and ritual purity."[242]

Thirdly, in the table-fellowship the Gentile believers observed certain basic food laws "prescribed by the Torah," e.g., they avoided pork and carefully investigated all the meat before using it in such fellowship to make sure that they had been properly slaughtered.[243] Dunn goes along with this third alternative since he sees it as fitting with the language of Galatians 2:11-14.[244] Therefore, for Dunn, Paul's confrontation with Peter was possibly because "by his action he had raised the ritual barriers surrounding their table-fellowship."[245]

Dunn further argues that the reason for Peter's withdrawal for the table-fellowship with the Gentiles is the question of Gentiles' purity status. James A. Fowler rightly opines that the Jewish concept of the table-fellowship regarded eating together as a "sign of oneness, equality, acceptance, commonality and intimacy within the Jewish covenant community."[246] Therefore, the issue that is at stake is certainly the Jewish Christians' attitude towards the Gentiles Christians' eating habit-i.e., distinctions based on the their food habits, which is visibly exemplified by Peter's withdrawal from the table-fellowship.

Therefore, Cephas may have concluded that given the theological presuppositions of the Jewish Christians he was expected to represent, his table fellowship was indefensible. In Paul's terms, Cephas "feared" the "political" consequences of

241 James D.G. Dunn, *Jesus, Paul and the Law* (London: SPCK, 1990), 151-159.

242 Dunn, *Jesus, Paul and the Law*, 152.

243 Dunn, *Jesus, Paul and the Law*, 153-154.

244 Dunn, *Jesus, Paul and the Law*, 154.

245 Dunn, *Jesus, Paul and the Law*, 154.

246 Dunn, *Jesus, Paul and the Law*, 154.

losing his position of power. Peter chose the position of power and denied his theological convictions.[247]

2.3 Paul's Response to Peter's Attitude (vv 14b-21)

Having evaluated the situation created by Peter's action and the Jewish Christians who followed him in verse 14a, Paul, now confronts Peter in an initial response.[248] According to Paul, in the previous course of action, Peter had abandoned his Jewish identity by living like a Gentile and not like a Jews by eating and had consequently declared that in Christ Jesus there is neither Jews nor Greek, clean or unclean.[249]

The term έ θνικῶς and Ί ουδαϊκῶς appear here as antithesis, employing a wide range of contrasts between practices typically Gentile and those typically Jewish.[250] In other words, it means "living according to Gentile and Jewish customs, particularly here with respect to the observance of the Jewish dietary laws-the former ignoring and later observing them."[251] Peter having free social access with the Gentiles suddenly turned back and began to disassociate with them. This conveys that he was practically compelling the Gentile Christians to 'Judaize.'[252]

The question arises: Why did Cephas fear a delegation from James and the Jerusalem church, when he himself was one of the "pillars" of that church? Were they Judaizers? Was James, who sent them, himself a Judaizer?[253] Or if not Judaizers, did they represent some conservative faction within the Jerusalem church

247 http://www.christinyou.net/galstag.html

248 Betz, *Galatians...*, 109.

249 εί σὔΙουδαῖος ὑπάρχων έθνικῶς καὶ οὐχῒΙουδαϊκῶς ζῇς, πῶς τάἔθνη άναγκάζεις ίουδαΐζειν; ("If you, being a Jew, live like the Gentiles and not like the Jews, how *is it that* you compel the Gentiles to live like Jews").

250 Paul F. Watson, *Paul, Judaism and the Gentiles: A Sociological Approach* (Cambridge: Cambridge University Press, 1986), 67.

251 James D.G. Dunn, *Jesus, Paul and the Law* (London: SPCK, 1990), 148.

252 Longenecker, "Galatians," *WBC*, 78.

253 F.F. Bruce, *The Epistle to the Galatians: A Commentary on the Greek Text* (Exeter: The Paternoster Press, 1982), 133.

that frightened Cephas by threatening to break off fellowship with Antioch Christians if their counsel was not heeded-counsel having to do with the need for Gentile believers at Antioch to observe the fourfold decree of Acts 15:20–21, 28–29 (assuming a North Galatian provenance), or having to do with the extension of the Jerusalem church's authority over Antiochian Christianity, or having to do with Peter's sphere of apostolic authority even at Antioch, or some combination of the above?[254]

Longnecker states the ἰουδαΐζειν ("to live as a Jews" or to live according to Jewish religious regulations) is plausibly the most important term of this sentence for grasping the nature of Paul's confrontation to Peter.[255] Ιουδαΐζειν, for Paul embodies "more than submitting to Jewish dietary laws; it describes forcing one to become a Jewish convert obliged to keep the whole Torah (cf. 5:3)."[256] Therefore Betz opines: "by attempting to preserve the integrity of the Jewish Christians as Jews, Cephas destroyed the integrity Gentile Christians as believer in Christ."[257] For Paul, Peter's inconsistency with his own earlier practice entirely contradicts justification which is achieved by Christ.

Paul reminds to Peter that social barriers on the basis of one's eating habits should not be root cause of disunity in the church. So, from verse 15 onwards Paul expresses his arguments on the Peter's attitude which is evidently the doctrine of "Justification by faith" rather than by "works of the Law." In verse 15 and 16, Paul gives a self-definition of Jewish Christians; first in terms of race and then in terms of theological commitment.[258] φύσει ("by nature") implies that Jewish Christians are defined first of all by the circumstance of birth.

This is better illuminated in the text phrase, ἐ θνῶ ν ἁμαρτωλοί, ("sinners of the Gentiles"), which is a usual Jewish way of

254 Bruce, *The Epistle to the Galatians…*, 133-134.

255 Bruce, *The Epistle to the Galatians…*, 133-134.

256 Longenecker, "Galatians," *WBC*, 78.

257 Betz, *Galatians…*, 112.

258 Betz, *Galatians...*, 112.

referring to Gentiles.[259] It shows the attitude of the Jews towards the Gentiles and here Paul's use probably carries with it a note of irony. Dunn observes that by this time in Jewish circles the word ἁμαρτωλοί has already developed a particularly Jewish flavor.[260]

Accordingly, the Jews commit sin when they transgress the Torah and can have forgiveness by following certain cultic means, whereas the Gentiles are sinners outside the Torah and therefore there is no forgiveness.[261] Therefore, Paul by mentioning their Jewish heritage aspires to attack Peter and other Jewish Christians who followed Peter taking the very basics of their understating. This becomes clearer in the following verse where he talks about the knowledge of both himself and the Jewish believers that they were "justified by faith in Jesus Christ" and not by the "works of the Law."

The verb δικαιοῦται ("justified") in v 16, predominantly Paul's word in the New Testament. In spite of its complexity in Pauline thought it is a metaphor drawn from the court to describe the judge's responsibility to give a fair verdict and to justify. To be 'justified' means to be formally recognized as 'righteous,' or to be in the right relation. However, there is a difference between the Hebrews and the Greek concept. The former Greek perceived it as an ideal norm by which particular claims or duties could be measured whereas the later it understood in terms of relation.[262] "To be justified means to be declared righteous before God, that is, to enjoy a status of being accepted by God."[263]

The Genitive phrases ἐξἔργων νόμου and ἐκπίστεως Χριστοῦ and its meaning are widely debated in modern Pauline

---

259 Longenecker, "Galatians," *WBC*, 83.

260 Karl H. Rengstrof, "ἁμαρτωλός" in *TDNT*, I (Grand Rapids: William B. Eerdmans Publishing Company, 1964), 332-333; D.R. de Lacey, "Gentiles," in *DPL* (Illinois: InterVarsity Press, 1993), 335-339; and P.A. Blair, "Gentiles," in *NBD*, 3rd ed. (Secunderabad: OM Books, 2000), 405.

261 Dunn, *Jesus, Paul and the Law*..., 150.

262 Betz, *Galatians*..., 115.

263 Dunn, *Jesus, Paul and the Law*..., 134.

scholarship.[264] John Barclay observes along with Dunn and others that "the problem here is not legalism but cultural imperialism-regarding Jewish identity and Jewish customs as the essential tokens of membership in the people of God."[265] Therefore, Paul makes it very clear that "works of the Law" are not the medium by which God justifies his people but through "faith in Christ."

The phrase ἐκπίστεως Χριστοῦ has been argued among the various scholars and its subjective genitival expression referring to the "faith or faithfulness of Christ Jesus," "the faith which Christ create in man by his revelation of God's love," "Christ's own faith" and "Christ tenure in *fideicommissum* of Roman testamentary law."[266]

Betz observes about this phrase is very interesting as he suggest the phrase for objective use i.e., faith in Christ. In his own words, "Believing that the messiah is Jesus becomes the channel which mediates 'justification' before the throne of God, instead of 'doing' the "works of the law" that is pre-Pauline understanding. " For the Apostle, 'faith in Christ Jesus' is faith in the crucifixion and resurrection of Christ which means being in Christ (Gal 2: 9-21; 3:26-28; 5:5-6, 24; 6:14)."[267]

Therefore, Paul, by responding to Peter's action wants the believers to carry on the common act of eating together which

---

264 Fung, *The Epistle to the Galatians*, 113.

265 T.R. Schreiner, "Works of the Law," in *DPL* (Illinois: InterVarsity Press, 1993), 975-979.

266 John Barclay, *Obeying the Truth: A Study of Paul's Ethics in Galatians* (Edinburgh: T&T Clark, 1988), 239. Barclay is building here on the insights of E.P. Sanders, Paul and Palestinian Judaism: A Comparison of Patterns of Religion (Philadelphia: Fortress Press, 1977); James D.G. Dunn, "The New Perspective on Paul," *BJRL* 65 (1983), 95-122; "The Incident at Antioch (Gal 2:11-18)," *JSNT* 18 (1983), 3-57; and Watson, Paul, Judaism and the Gentiles..., 68.

267 Fung, *The Epistle to the Galatians*, 114-115; Betz, *Galatians...*, 117; Richard N. Longenecker, "Galatians," *WBC*, 83; however, they all supported the objective interpretation of the phrase.

denies any visible distinction between Jewish and Gentile Christians, between circumcised and uncircumcised.[268]

In vv 17-20, Paul for the greater part argues that the law plays no positive role in Christian living but rather that the Christians life is lived in Christ. In verse 18, Paul once again explains his theological conviction keeping Peter's action that if someone follows the law becomes a transgressor.[269] Further he makes clear in vv 19-20 that the Jewish believers need not fear being labeled sinners by the law, because in Christ they have died to any relationship with law. Therefore, he states that there should not be any difference among the believers based on their identities.

In v 21, he gave a direct statement refuting the change made against him with an explanatory sentence that identifies the crux of the matter.[270] Paul, therefore, argues that since Christ did not die in vain, righteousness cannot be attained through the law. It is purely through faith in Christ and only by His grace alone. It is not human achievement but God's free gift received through faith in Him.[271]

2.4 Historical Analysis of the Incident at Antioch

the Antioch episode most likely took place *after* Paul and Barnabas returned to Syrian Antioch from their mission to Cyprus and southern Galatia as recorded by Luke in Acts 13:4–14:25, *during* the time when "they stayed there [at Antioch] a long time with the disciples" as told us in Acts 14:26–28, and *before* the Jerusalem Council of Acts 15:1–29.[272]

Furthermore, while Luke tells us how the church at Antioch was founded (cf. Acts 11:20–26), we know very little about its

268 Betz, *Galatians...*, 117; Dunn, *The Theology of Paul to the Galatians...* 149.

269 J.H. Schutz, *Paul and the Anatomy of Apostolic Authority* (Cambridge: Cambridge University Press, 1975), 150.

270 Bruce, *The Epistles to the Galatians...*, 142.

271 Betz, *Galatians...*, 126.

272 E.P. Sanders, *Paul, the Law and the Jewish People* (Philadelphia: Fortress Press, 1983), 27.

character and nothing of its physical circumstances. Was it one congregation made up of both Jewish and Gentile believers? Were there two congregations, one Jewish and the other Gentile? Or were there a number of congregations meeting at various places in the city, some ethnically mixed and others not? The impression given by Paul is of one group composed of both Jews and Gentiles, and such an impression seems in line with what we know of Jewish-Gentile relations at Antioch at the time. Yet it could just as well be that there were a number of groups of believers at Antioch, with some of mixed ethnic character and others not, and that what took place in one of the groups affected them all.[273]

The importance of the Antioch episode for an understanding of the development of early Christianity is highlighted by the many diverse interpretations given it during the first five centuries of Christian history. The Ebionites, for example, made it the basis for an attack on Paul, Marcion, on the other hand, used it to attack Peter and to prove the direct antagonism of Christianity to everything Jewish.[274] And early critics of Christianity, such as Celsus (late second century) and Porphyry (c 230–305), seem to have frequently used this incident to assail the Christian faith itself, impugning the characters of both Paul and Peter for their shameful quarreling.[275]

Within the mainstream of Gentile Christendom, Tertullian, arguing against the Marcionites, took the confrontation of Peter to be an overreaction on Paul's part; Clement of Alexandria asserted that "Cephas" here was not Cephas the apostle, the one called by Jesus "Peter," but one of the seventy apostles bearing the same name; while Origen, Chrysostom, and Jerome saw it as a staged event concocted between Peter and Paul in order to bring the issues out into the open and so to condemn the Judaizers more effectively.[276]

273 Longenecker, "Galatians," *WBC*, 71.

274 Longenecker, "Galatians," *WBC*, 72.

275 Longenecker, "Galatians," *WBC*, 64.

276 Longenecker, "Galatians," *WBC*, 64.

Augustine, however, in direct opposition to Jerome, interpreted it as a case of the higher claims of truth over rank and office-of Peter's error despite his primacy, of Paul's rightful confrontation and defense of the gospel, and of Peter's humility in accepting correction from an inferior in both age and standing.[277]

2.5 Evaluation of Texts

2.5.1 Paul's Second Visit to Jerusalem (Gal 2: 1-10)

We need to discover the relationship between Paul and Jerusalem according to Galatians 1 and 2. Verbs such as ά νεθέ μην which means *lay a matter before someone for consideration* suggests that Paul went up again Jerusalem after fourteen years and laid before the pillars of Jerusalem the gospel which he preaches among the Gentiles.[278] BAGD[279] defines this verb well: 'declare, communicate, and refer with the added idea that the person to whom a thing is referred is asked for his opinion, lay something before someone for consideration.' But does this verb tell anything before the relationship between the two parties involved? In particular, does it have any overtone of submitting to a higher authority an issue which the one making the submission was incompetent to resolve on his own? Does Paul's use of the word amount to an acknowledgement on his part that the authority of his gospel depended on Jerusalem's approval?[280]

Moreover, Paul goes out his way to point out that he went up in accordance with revelation. Furthermore, he calls the Jerusalem leadership 'men of repute', a phrase which acknowledges the high standing in which pillars apostles were having authority.[281] However, how is it that Paul in the same breath can both assert his independence of the Jerusalem apostles and yet also acknowledge

277 Longenecker, "Galatians," *WBC*, 64.

278 Longenecker, "Galatians," *WBC*, 64.

279 Longenecker, "Galatians," *WBC*, 64-65.

280 James D.G. Dunn, *Jesus, Paul and the Law* (London: SPCK, 1990), 113.

281 W. Bauer, *A Greek-English Lexicon of the New Testament and Other Early Christian Literature*, ET, ed. W.F. Arndt and F.W. Gingrich; 2nd rev. ed. F. W. Gingrich and F.W Danker (University of Chicago, 1979).

that the effectiveness of his work depended on their approval of his gospel? Nor does it seem to meet the force of Gal 2:2 to argue that Paul's concern was simply for the future unity of the church.[282]

In short, the purpose of His second visit to Jerusalem was, in laying his gospel before the Jerusalem apostles what he sought was not so much their approval as their recognition of his gospel's validity.[283] Regarding Paul's relationship with Jerusalem apostles we draw three major points:

a) Paul maintains the independence of his gospel and apostleship as to its validity and authority.[284]
b) Paul acknowledges his earlier dependence on the Jerusalem leadership.[285]
c) By the time Paul wrote Galatians he was no longer prepared to acknowledge the authority of Jerusalem to the same extent.[286]

To Sum up, Paul's second visit to Jerusalem was particularly significant and Paul's purpose was evidently to secure the backing of the accepted leadership in Jerusalem for his Circumcision-free gospel to the gentiles.

2.5.2 A Betrayal of the Gospel of Christ

Paul adopted the cross as the center post of his Gospel. The gospel that Paul taught to the Galatians is consistent with that characteristic of Jesus Christ.[287] On account of perversion of the truth of the Gospel by the agitators, Galatians apparently put the Lord Jesus Christ and works-righteousness in juxtaposition for access to God or inheritance of the bliss through Abraham.[288]

---

282 James D.G. Dunn, *Jesus, Paul and the Law* (London: SPCK, 1990), 113.

283 Dunn, *Jesus, Paul and the Law*, 114.

284 Dunn, *Jesus, Paul and the Law*, 114-115.

285 Dunn, *Jesus, Paul and the Law*, 116.

286 Dunn, *Jesus, Paul and the Law*, 118.

287 Dunn, *Jesus, Paul and the Law*, 119.

288 Dunn, *Jesus, Paul and the Law*, 121.

K. James Carl says, "The soteriology of Galatians turned out such that they seemed to have believed in the restoration of broken relationship with God not by justification by grace through faith in Jesus Christ alone, but through merit acquired by their observation of the law and rituals."[289] Galatians were mixed up regarding the way of salvation by their synthesis of faith and works. They were not sure whether the gift of the Holy Spirit was by their works or by their hearing with faith. Paul asks the Galatians how they could turn back to the weak and beggarly elements. Therefore, it is evident that there was a betrayal of the gospel of Christ.

2.5.3 Pauline View of Freedom

Freedom is the integration of self in mind and action. Freedom means dealing with one's own limitations without illusion.[290] Freedom from fear, want, and oppression: all these are legitimate freedoms, valued and sought throughout the ages. John Stuart mill wrote that freedom chooses to escape the despotism of custom.[291] Thereby, how do we usually see freedom in Galatians? Paul accused the Galatians of slavery to the present age which was unforgiving, eager to predict future failure, unloving and the present age defeats ethics with moralism.

Therefore, by looking such context, Paul advocates, "freedom in Christ leaves us totally responsible for our behavior towards self and neighbor."[292] Paul vehemently argues that rejection of freedom and its attendant responsibility is a human problem. He says that, "but freedom is frightening. It involves responsibility that tests our strength and patience and faith."[293]

289 Jerry D. Benjamin, *For Freedom: Studies on Galatians* (Franklin, Tennessee: Providence House Publishers, 1993), 48.

290 K. James Carl, *The Pauline view of Christian Freedom* (Madras: The United Evangelical Lutheran Church), 42.

291 Carl, *The Pauline View...*, 42.

292 Jerry D. Benjamin, *For Freedom: Studies on Galatians* (Franklin, Tennessee: Providence House Publishers, 1993), 102.

293 Benjamin, *For Freedom...*, 11-12.

In Gal 5:1-12 Paul addressed people who had chosen unfreedom over freedom, who had heard the gospel and chosen nominal Christianity while submitting to the yoke of slavery to power and authority on earth.[294] For Paul, to be free is to take initiative. To be free is to choose. To be free is to act more than react. To be free is to believe God's promise and go on with life based on that promise. To be free from the law is to be empowered by the Spirit to do righteous work.[295] Therefore, we are free when we decide most things, but the reality of human limitation is such that we never decide everything. For Paul, "life in Christ is life in freedom."[296]

2.5.4 Theological Debate in Gal 2:11-21

In the recent decades the issues have become more historical than ecclesiastical, with the earlier exegetical assumptions being regularly and sharply questioned. In Particular, can we assume that Peter accepted Paul's confrontation and amended his conduct? If he did not, what does that tell us about the development of Paul's missionary work, about his subsequent relations with Jerusalem and Peter, about factions within first century Christianity?[297] Again, where does the Antioch incident fit within the history of that period? Can we assume that it formed the sequel to the Jerusalem council recommended Luke in Acts? Or is the issue more complex, with the historicity of Acts being called in questions in part at least by Paul's account?[298]

Secondly, dawn to centuries, Commentators and historians have raised question that what was the nature of the table-fellowship that Peter enjoyed with the Gentile believers? What was involved in it? What precisely did he withdraw from when the men from James arrived? The ready assumption laid close to

294 Benjamin, *For Freedom...*, 20-22.

295 Benjamin, *For Freedom...*, 74.

296 Benjamin, *For Freedom...*, 87.

297 Benjamin, *For Freedom...*, 88.

298 K. James Carl, *The Pauline view of Christian Freedom* (Madras: The United Evangelical Lutheran Church), 73.

hand that it was all simple a matter of the Jewish food laws.[299] The relationship between the church in Jerusalem and the church Antioch is significant to understand the conflict at Antioch. K. Stendahl says that here Paul's concern is not the salvation rather relationship between Jews and Gentile.[300]

The main argument of Paul in Galatians is about how one becomes Abraham's offspring, heir of his blessings is sufficient indication of the limits within which both sides had carried on the earlier debate. Thirdly, circumcision was only aspect of that debate.

The question discussed at the meeting in Jerusalem was not primarily whether Paul were apostles, but whether as apostles of Antioch, their practice of not circumcising their converts should continue without modification. Moreover, during the first century period the socio-political situation that confronts Judaism puts pressure on the infant churches. Wherever, this new Jewish sect's belief or practice was perceived to be a threat to Jewish institutions and traditions its members would almost certainly come under pressure from their fellow Jews to remain loyal to their unique Jewish heritage.[301] The mission of the men from James would have been their reaction to that threat.[302]

2.6 The Limits of Table- Fellowship in the Judaism of the Late Second Temple Period

The significance of table–fellowship in the east is well known. In Judaism particularly the religious significance of shared meal was central. 'In Judaism', as Jeremias notes, 'Table –fellowship means fellowship before God, for the eating of a piece of broken bread by everyone who shares in the meal brings out the fact that they

---

299 F.C. Baur, *Paul: His Life and Works* (London: Williams & Norgate, 1873), 133-136.

300 W.W. Gasque, *A History of the Criticism of the Acts of the Apostles* (Grand Rapids: William B. Eerdmans Publishing Company, 1975), 77-79.

301 E.D. Burton, *Galatians* (Edinburgh: T&T Clark, 1921), 104.

302 K. Stendahl, 'The Apostle Paul and the Introspective conscience of the West', *Harvard Theological Review 56* (1963), 199-215.

all have a share in the blessing which the master of the house has spoken over unbroken bread.'[303]

There were some limits based on which Jews decided who can partake in table-fellowship. These limits would be determined partly by explicit laws in the Torah, particularly concerning unclean foods (Lev11:1-23; Deut 14: 3-21) and in differing degrees by the multiplying *halakoth* of the oral tradition concerning tithes and ritual purity.[304] Obedience to the law on unclean foods had been one of the make or break issues in the Maccabean revolt (1Macc 1:62-63).

There were some fundamental laws which were a limiting factor for considerable consequence for the devout Jew's practice of table-fellowship. The purity ritual and tithing were among them. Therefore, what was it that the men from James objected to or found fault with in the table-fellowship at Antioch? And how could that defect be remedied, if at all? Or what was involved in the table-fellowship at Antioch before the men from James appeared? How strict was the discipline of diet or ritual purity into which Peter and others withdraw? On what terms could the table-fellowship have been reassumed thereafter?

All that the evidence warrants is that a delegation from the Jerusalem church arrived at Antioch, probably sent by James to express certain practical concerns of Jerusalem believers regarding the expression of the Christian faith at Antioch, and that the arrival of these men and their statement of the Jerusalem church's concerns served to trigger Peter's withdrawal from table fellowship with Gentile believers at Antioch.[305]

2.7 Theology of Ethics in Paul

Basic to the ethical teaching of the bible is the insistence that the final measure for human conduct is not to be derived from

303 James D.G. Dunn, *Jesus, Paul and the Law* (London: SPCK, 1990), 135.

304 R. Jewett, 'The Agitators and the Galatians Congregation,' *New Testament Studies* 17 (1970-71), 204-206.

305 J. Jeremias, *New Testament Theology*. Vol.1: The Proclamation of Jesus (London: SCM Press, 1971), 115.

individuals but stems from the nature of God, from the quality of his love for humankind, and from the character of his redemptive activity.[306]

2.7.1 The Background of Pauline Ethics

To begin with, Paul's heritage is at least partly Jewish. He identifies himself emphatically with the people of Israel and speaks of the Pharisaic attitude toward the law which had characterized his pre-conversion life (Phil 3:4-6). His belonging to Abraham's people is further stresses in 2Cor 11:22, and in Gal 1:13-14 he refers to his past zeal for the traditions of Judaism. Indeed, the whole of Romans 9-11 is a poignant testimony to the extent to which, even as a Christian, the apostle feels himself bound to the people of God.[307]

As such his ethical outlook also is more or less influenced by his background. To the Jews, morals and religion are one: "Ethics is the soul of Jewish religion."[308] All his letters attest his indebtedness to the faith of the Old Testament and to the traditions of this covenant people. Therefore, it would be impossible to understand the Pauline gospel apart from the apostle's Jewish heritage (2Cor 9:1).[309]

Again Paul must have used the apocryphal books. For in Paul's days, they were used in association with the more strictly canonical Old Testament books, namely Tobit, IV Esdras, I Enoch etc. thus, D.C. Simpson believes that Paul did in fact employ materials from exactly these portions of Tobit. However, Furnish Paul argued that instated of using apocryphal book namely Tobit,

---

306 James D.G. Dunn, *Jesus, Paul and the Law* (London: SPCK, 1990), 137.

307 Longenecker, "Galatians," *WBC*, 73.

308 Richard N. Longenecker, "New Testament Social Ethics for Today," in Brian S. Rosner, ed. *Understanding Paul's Ethics: Twentieth Century Approaches* (Grand Rapids, Michigan: William B. Eerdmans Publishing Company, 1995), 345.

309 Victor Paul Furnish, *Theology and Ethics in Paul* (New York: Abingdon Press, 1968), 28.

Paul might have derived from Proverbs and other moral literature of the time.[310]

Moreover, one must consider the possibility that Paul's ethical teaching is in some measure dependent upon the traditions of Rabbinic Judaism as "most of his theology and his anthropology clearly reveals his Jewish background."[311] In this regard, W.D. Davies suggests that the apostles met the need for ethical regulations within his congregations by framing for them moral codes using Jewish hortatory materials.[312]

Another factor that cannot be ignored is Hellenistic influence on Paul. There are no explicit references to secular sources in the Pauline corpus, yet his ethical teaching is indebted to Hellenistic sources in a more general way. In his writings phrases and types of thought to the writings of Greek moralists of that period, chiefly Stoic is readily recognized.[313] Furthermore, we cannot, again ignore the relation of Paul's ethical teaching to the ethical teaching of Jesus. It is established that Paul's traditions included saying of Jesus for on occasion he specially cites these.[314]

Some scholars even go further that Paul collected the words of Jesus and the apostle himself "must have shared in and contributed to" the attempt to preserve those saying…"[315] For Example, Paul's exhortation to the married that they should not divorce (1Cor 10-11), although the possibility of such in nonetheless acknowledge in v. 11a) is specially identified as coming from "the Lord" and reflects similar traditions incorporated in the synoptic gospels (Matt 5:32; 19:9; Mark 10:11-12; Luke 16:18).[316]

---

310 Orton Scott Enslin, *The Ethics of Paul* (New York: Harper and Brothers, 1930), 1.

311 Furnish, *Theology and Ethics in Paul*, 29.

312 Furnish, *Theology and Ethics in Paul*, 35.

313 Joseph A, Fitzmyer, *Pauline Theology: A Brief Sketch* (New Jersey: Prentice Hall, Inc., 1967), 7.

314 Furnish, *Theology and Ethics in Paul*, 38.

315 Enslin, *The Ethics of Paul*, 17.

316 Furnish, *Theology and Ethics in Paul*, 52.

Therefore, one must remember that the background against which Paul wrote his letters is pluralistic and complex.

2.7.2 The Theological Structure of Paul's Ethic

2.7.2.1 Indicative and Imperative

God's saving act in Christ's death and resurrection is the ground of ethical appeal for Paul. "The old Yeast" of vice must be cleaned out "in order that you may be a fresh batch just as you are, without fermentation, because Christ our Paschal Lamb was sacrificed" (1Cor 5:7). Ethical behavior is to correspond to what God has enabled them to be through Christ's sacrifice. This ethical appeal has been called the "indicative and imperative" that is, "become in your character the conduct what God's action in Christ has made you to be."[317] In the light of his own exegesis Ridderbos defines what is meant by these grammatical terms in Paul's Theology.

> What is meant is that the new life in its moral manifestation is at one time proclaimed and posited as the fruit of the redemptive work of God in Christ through the Holy Spirit-the indicative; elsewhere, however, it is put with no less force as a categorical demand-the imperative.[318]

As for the relationship of Christ's death and resurrection is concerned, the indicative is here fundamental, that those who are in Christ have died to sin (Rom 6:2). This whole pronouncement, however, is directed towards stimulating human responsibility and arousing to activity; "Let not sin therefore reign in your mortal body… and do not present your members any longer as weapons of unrighteousness in the service of sin…" (Rom 6:12, 13).[319]

There were a long debate about the indicative and imperative as to whether they were an aspect of Paul's total ethical presentation.

---

317 Furnish, *Theology and Ethics in Paul*, 56.

318 Furnish, *Theology and Ethics in Paul*, 52.

319 S.C. Mott, "Ethics" in *Dictionary of Paul and His Letters,* edited by Gerald F. Hawthorne, Ralph P. Martin and Daniel G. Reid (Leicester: InterVarsity Press, 1993), 269-275.

The debate is mostly between Paul Werne and Hermann Jacoby. The former states that the indicative is expressed in Paul by speaking of the Holy Spirit as the power which takes man from this world and transfer him into a higher world. However, concerning the imperative, he says that the Spirit is a high, divine potentially in man in which the Christian himself participates in the road to victory.

He concludes that we have an ethic of miracle and an ethic of will here quite abruptly merged into one another. Jacoby stated that the imperative is used by Paul as exhortation for man to accomplish in fact what God's grace had accomplished in principle (indicative).... Christians are engaged in an "ethical process" in which during their Christian life, they actually become what they are in principle.[320]

However, in 1924 Rudolf Bultmann wrote an article in which he focused upon the theological aspect of Paul's ethics. In an attempt to grasp the structure of Paul's theological ethics, Bultmann described the indicative and the imperative as the basic structure of Pauline ethics. Anyway, the imperative is not a secondary application of the gospel designed for the spiritual immature.

Betz suggests that in Paul's early letters, as in 1 Thessalonians, ethics was a means of preserving the present state of holiness up to the Day of Judgment (1Thess 5:23). Certainly by the time of Paul's writing Romans the connection of the imperative to the indicative clearly had become implicit. In Romans 6 union with Christ (Rom 6: 2-11) compels behavior which is consistent with it (Rom 6: 12-13). In Philippians, Paul invokes participation in the ethos of the drama of salvation which is at the basis as believers.[321]

---

320 Herman Ridderbos, *Paul: An Outline of His Theology,* translated by John Richard Dewitt (Grand Rapids: William B. Eerdmans Publishing Company, 1975), 253.

321 Ridderbos, *Paul: An Outline of His Theology...*, 254.

2.7.3 The Three Basic Motifs of Pauline Ethic

Any study of the ethic of Paul must acknowledge that multiple theological motifs have left their mark upon the ethic. If one seeks to analyses the structure of Paul's ethic in terms of its absolutely fundamental components, the Pauline ethic is compounded of the apostle's theological, eschatological and Christological convictions. These are the three inseparably related root-motifs of his preaching and thus, also, of his ethic.[322]

2.7.3.1 Theological

The Paulineethic is first of all radically theological because it presupposes that man's whole life and being is independent upon the sovereign, creative and redemptive power of God. On this basis, Paul asked the Corinthians what they possess that was not given to them. He said, "If then you really received it all as a gift, why take the credit to yourselfʼ" (1Cor 4:7). So, Pauline theology is radically theocentric. The theme of God's power pervades his whole theology. To Paul, transcendent power is God's alone (IICor 4:7). It is God's power to create and redeem which enables faith to be faith (Rom 4:16-21). That is why the apostle may describe his gospel of justification as the power of God for salvation to all who believe (Rom 1:16), thereby, making it a gospel of justification through God's grace received by faith.[323]

The spirit which God bestows (Rom 5:5) is God's power at work within and among the believers. But most of the gracious saving power is revealed in Christ (1Cor 1:24; 5:4; 2Cor 12:9). And the redemption from the bondage of sin is through Christ. As such, those who are in Christ will also be raised by the power of God (1Cor 6:14). In the end, God alone will reign and everything is and will be God's and his alone, even Christ (1Cor 3:23).

---

322 William D. Dennison, "Indicative and Imperative: The Basic Structure of Pauline Ethics" in *Calvin Theological Journal*, Vol. 14 (April 1979-November 1997), 58.

323 Dennison, "Indicative and Imperative..., 58-59.

2.7.3.2 Eschatological

Secondly, Pauline ethic is thoroughly eschatological. His eschatology is a fundamental perspective with which everything else is viewed. He does not express the absolute sovereignty of God not only in the spatially conceived mythology of God's dwelling in heaven, but also in the temporally conceived mythology of God's future triumph over all hostile powers. Yet, Pauline eschatology is not totally futuristic. His eschatological action of God has also a present dimension.

The whole point is – what is given is present in its fullness, although there is still something not given-namely resurrection from the death and the final cosmic triumph of God's power over death. Thus, the importance of the eschatological orientation of Pauline theology for the apostle's ethic in particular is well exhibited in Rom 12-13. The appeal not to be conformed to this age (Rom 12:2) presupposes the believer's belonging to another age in which, through faith, he already participates.[324]

2.7.3.3 Christological

To Paul faith in God's power is focused and defined in commitment to Christ. For Paul, the resurrection brought Christ into a new relationship with human who have faith.[325] And that God's power has been operative in human's history and those who belong to him, who participate in his body, have been freed from sin's domination. When Paul speaks of life in Christ, he is speaking of life made new by the love of God bestowed in Christ and by that very fact claimed by God, held in custody by God's love given in Christ.

Romans 6th chapter is one of the crucial chapters for determining the Christological dimensions of Pauline theology in general and the Pauline ethic in particular. Baptism is the sign that the believer has already has dies with Christ; it is baptism "into death in order that, just as Christ was raised from the dead

324 Furnish, *Theology and Ethics in Paul*, 213.

325 Furnish, *Theology and Ethics in Paul*, 213.

though the glory of God, so we too might walk in newness of life (Rom 6:4). Hence, the believer's life is not just analogous to the future resurrection life, but already shows it forth. Paul's understanding is also derives from his Christology. By one man's obedience, those who belong to him by believing in him are given life and righteousness, Christ's obedience unto death (Phil 2:8) is regarded as the ultimate expression of humble concern for others. Moreover, Paul intends Christ's obedience to be pragmatic for the believers. What he has done becomes an incentive imperative and encouragement, thus, the believer's obedience is made possible and imperative by God's working within and among them, its character is to be part of Christ's own obedience.

2.7.4 Central Place of Morality

According to Paul, love is the specific pattern of life by which grace forms the new reality of the believer. Love as a central place of morality is a distinguishing and the most consistent feature of Paul's moral instruction. While love plays a minor role in Greek ethical theory and a significant role in Jewish *paraenesis*, the centrality of this theme is unique in Paul, who maintains that love is the fulfillment of the law (Rom 13:8, 10; Gal 5:14).[326] The super natural infusion of love through the Holy Spirit produces the character upon which eschatological hope above the final judgment of God is built (Rom 5:3-5).[327]

The most significant question in current scholarship pertinent to Pauline ethics is the place of the law. Love gives full expression to the law (Gal 5:14) as we bear each other's burdens and thus fulfill the law of Christ (Gal 6:2). Some would suggest that the law is no longer pertinent as a moral authority. The believer has been freed to consider all kinds of ethical traditions, shifting them by the law of faith and love. However, love is not a replacement of law, but a new motivation, understanding and power for meeting and surpassing its moral demands.

---

326 Furnish, *Theology and Ethics in Paul*, 215.

327 Fitzmyer, *Pauline Theology...*, 40.

The combination is crucial. Obedient deeds of justice and self sacrifice which requirement of the law, which is in tune with love remains as a standard of righteous living, that provides a pattern, warning, instruction and exhortation, including matters as specific as sexual immorality and remuneration of leaders (1Cor 9:10; 10: 6-11).[328]

The law of Christ is the criterion of love which fulfils the law as it makes that obedience possible. For example, the obligation in the law of responsibility to the poor is carried out through the grace of God flowing through the believers (2Cor 9:0-10).

2.7.5 Social Ethic as well as Community Ethic

One of the major themes of Galatians epistle is the question of social ethics (Gal 5:13-6:10). The question is, if Christians rejected the law, were they not also rejecting the morality which it represented? Paul's reply in Galatians is a definite 'no'. To him, those who rejected the law out of Christian convictions had rejected only the outward from the morality, which could never ultimately make a man completely righteous anyway. The Christian now has the Spirit of Christ within him, which is both a 'law' in the sense that it is a principle of action, and also a source of moral strength and ability. Although the Christian gospel lays down no specific imperatives, 'those who belong to Christ Jesus have crucifies the body with its passions and desires' (v. 24), and so their moral directives are formulated by the fruit of the Holy Spirit which manifest itself in their lives.[329] Morality is not judged by rules and regulations, but according to the kind of existence a man has, whether dominated by body or Spirit. The main emphasis here is on the person of Jesus Christ and his indwelling in the life of the Christian.

In 2 Corinthians 8-9, Paul's social concern is limited to the church. Hence, his ethic of sharing is a community ethic, not a social ethic. The collection was directed to the poor of the saints

328 James W. Thompson, *Moral Formation according to Paul* (Grand Rapids, Michigan: Baker Academic, 2011), 209.

329 Mott, "Ethics"..., 272.

(2Cor 8: 4; Rom 15:26). The givers indeed will be praised for their "liberality of sharing to them and to all (2Cor 9:13; Gal 6:10). Does this broader designation denote needy people in general, or only the needy among the all Christians?

Indication of more universal reference is found in other texts which apply to non-believers. In Gal 6:10, Paul concludes his discussion of giving with the admonition, "Do well to all people, but especially to the household of faith." The first part of the phrase is the general principle, followed by the specific application to the church. Loving service to the needy non-believers is also evident in Rom 12:13-14. Paul enjoins hospitality in its literal sense of love for one or care of strangers, here meaning non- believers since it contrasts the immediately preceding injunction of sharing with fellow Christians and the following stipulation of love to one's enemies.

Summary

Paul's exposure of Peter's eating habits and Paul's response to Peter's attitude shows that Paul advocates freedom for Jewish with regard to circumcision and partaking in Lord's Table. Paul confronts Peter and reminds him that his hypocrisy could be destructive factor for the new Converts. There are various interpretations have been given to 'eating together' however, mostly scholar argue that it could be social gather or Lord's Table. This chapter evaluate the text and it background to find out the root cause of the problem that was false teaching in the church and secondly issue of Apostleship of Paul. How did Jerusalem council impact on the Antioch's incident have been explained that it was the Pillars from Jerusalem who were behind the conflict?

In the ethical instructions Paul made use of the traditional material drawn from his Jewish background as well as from Hellenistic presuppositions. But he integrated that material into his preaching of the gospel in order to explain what it meant to conduct one's life in a Christian manner. Confronted with different situations in his churches, the apostle shaped his arguments in the context of his theology. His teaching was not characterized by the elaboration of the theoretical system of thought but was unfolded as he answered concrete questions and thus explained the central meaning of the good news and its implications for the behavior of those who believe in Christ.[330]

One can see now that the ethical theme of Paul contends that what the law can never do, through the weakness of human nature, "the rule of the Spirit of life in Christ Jesus" does accomplish, so that the law is fulfilled in us (Rom 8:1-4). Paul spells out the effect of this identification as producing the Christ like-character-the fruit of the Holy Spirit-in every willing behavior (Gal 5:22-23; Rom 5:5; 8:9-14). This transformation of men by inner dynamic of the Christ spirit is one of the central ethical motifs of Christianity.

330 Mott, "Ethics"..., 272.

Chapter 3

Pauline Christological and Missiological Framework and His Gentiles Mission

Introduction

Paul's presentation of Jesus Christ differs in a radical way from the presentations in the Gospels. The vital difference was made by the resurrection of Jesus. The unfolding of the suffering Messiah in the Gospels becomes the triumphant living Christ of the epistles, but he is no less Messiah. When Paul writes about Jesus Christ, the messianic mission has been accomplished. He develops his own reflections on the new-look messianic concept, which found fulfillment in the risen Christ, who inaugurated a spiritual kingdom. Pauline Christology has been frequently discussed under the heading of the prominent titles Paul employed -Christ, Lord, Son of God, Saviour- and the prominent analogies such as Adam and wisdom.

However, these titles do not engage the full picture of Pauline Christology.[331] To know more about Pauline Christology one

331 John W. Drane, "Tradition, Law and ethics in Pauline Theology" in *Novum Testamentum*, Vol. XVI (January, 1974): 172.

should find out the origin of Paul's Christology, its narrative framework, its dual focus on the Divinity and Humanity of Christ. This chapter is an attempt to understand all features related to Christology in Pauline corpus. Second part of the paper discusses Paul's corporate Christology and Christian identity. The essence of Paul's view of Christ lies in the assertion that God has made Christ the victor over the power of sin.[332]

3.1 The Origins of Paul's Christology

3.1.1 Judaism

One approach is to attempt to extrapolate from the New Testament document and extracanonical sources Paul the Pharisee's beliefs about the coming Messiah. How much influence did Paul Christology owe to his pre-Christian messianic beliefs? This issue, however, involves a huge amount of conjecture not only about messianic faith in pre-70 A.D. but also Paul's unique appropriation of his heritage in Pharisaic faith. Unfortunately, apart from a new reference here and there, Paul says little about his pre-Christian beliefs about Messiah. The most one can assume, judging from a text such as Rom 9:5, is that he must have believed in a coming human and Davidic Messiah. While Paul's debate to Jewish Messianism, and Particularly Pharisaic Messianism, was surely greater than this, the evidence for discovering the degree or character of this debate is not available.[333]

3.1.2 Hellenism

This is another method to know the origin of Paul's Christology named as "History-of-religions" (*religionsgeschichtliche*) approach. The influential example of this approach is W. Bousser's

332 Eduard Lohse, "Changes of Thought in Pauline Theology? Some Reflections on Paul's Ethical Teachings in the Context of His Theology," in *Theology and Ethics in Paul and His Interpreters: Essays in Honor of Victor Paul Furnish*, Eugene H. Lovering Jr. and Jerry L. Sumney, eds. (Nashville: Abingdon Press, 1996), 146.

333 Gerald F. Hawthrone and Ralph P. Martin, *Dictionary of Paul and His Letters* (Leicester: InterVarsity Press, 1993), 100.

classic work *Kyrios Christos* (1913). There the Christology of Paul and the early church are compared with ideas from the Greco-Roman world, particularly those found in its various forms of Pagan religious thought. For instance, it was assumed that Paul appropriated the title *Kyrios* from pagan usage and so related the Hellenizing influence on the early Christian thought. One significant aspect of this approach, however, assumes a radical distinction between Hellenism and Palestinian Judaism, an assumption that has severely described by the work of M. Hengel and others. Research has shown, for instance, that document such as Sirach and the Maccabean corpus attest to the influence of Hellenism on Palestinian Jewish thinking about God and other religious matters well before the Christian era.[334]

3.2 Paul's Conversion/ Call and Early Christian Tradition

Another approach arises from the Paul's own letters and in exploring Paul's own statement about his call/ conversion. From this evidence insights may be drawn about how that experience and his encounter with early Christian confessions may have shaped his Christology. Galatians 1:11-23 provides Paul's statement about his conversion; he claims that gospel which he received is revelation from God. The incident recorded in Acts and his letters may contradict to each other, however, it is clear that Paul did not see his commission, mission and essential message as deriving from a human source.[335] Paul presents significant pictures of Christ in various ways such as: (1) The Gospel of Christ;[336] the content of Paul's gospel is an issue in Galatians which he identifies with "the gospel of Christ," (2) the Risen and Exalted Christ, (3) The Corporate Christ, (4) The Saviour Christ.

334 Donald Guthrie, *New Testament Theology* (London: InterVarsity Press, 1981), 248.

335 Hawthrone, *Dictionary of Paul and His Letters*, 100.

336 Hawthrone, *Dictionary of Paul and His Letters*, 100-101.

3.3 The Narrative Framework of Paul's Christology

The universe of Paul's thought revolved around the Son of God, Jesus Christ. Paul's Christology illumined his thought in its entirely, sometime shedding its light on aspects of his thought that one might have expected would have gone relatively untouched by Christology.[337] The narrative framework of Pauline Christology is based on four aspects such as: (1) The Story of Christ, (2) The Story of Israel, (3) The Story of the World, (4) The Story of God.

3.4 The Divinity and Humanity of Jesus Christ in Paul's Christology

3.4.1 Christ's Divinity

3.4.1.1 "Christ... the Wisdom of God"

Paul spoke of Jesus both as the wisdom of God, as an agent in creation (1Cor 1:24, 30; 8:6; Col 1: 15-17) and as the one who accompanied Israel as the "Rock" in the wilderness (1Cor 10:4). The full flower of this Christological wisdom thinking came to expression in the hymn in Colossians 1: 15-20 where Christ is said to be the image of the invisible God, the firstborn of creation, and the means and goal of creation.[338] The term Χριστοῦ is the most frequent 'title' applied to Jesus by Paul. In the genuine Pauline letters it occurs some 270 times.[339] Firstly, Paul's references to Jesus as "Christ" serve to remind readers of Jesus' humanity, especially His role as the Jewish Messiah. When Paul listed for the Romans some distinctive privileges of Israel as the people of God, he concluded by noting that "from them is traced the human ancestry of Christ" (Rom. 9:5; cf. Eph. 2:12).

This affirmation was also made earlier in the letter (Rom. 1:3) when Paul connected his proclamation of the gospel with the fulfillment of promises regarding Christ made by Old Testament prophets. The fulfillment of the prophetic statements about Christ

337 Hawthrone, *Dictionary of Paul and His Letters*, 100-101.

338 Hawthrone, *Dictionary of Paul and His Letters*, 101-102.

339 Hawthrone, *Dictionary of Paul and His Letters*, 102-103.

was important to Paul because he found in them assurance for Israel's salvation. As he wrote later in this letter, citing Isaiah 59:20; The deliverer will come from Zion; he will turn godlessness away from Jacob" (Rom. 11:26). Paul looked forward to the day when Israel would receive Jesus as Christ.[340]

Paul takes the traditional uses of the title with respect especially to the death and resurrection of Jesus. The distinct Pauline element comes out in the use of the phrase 'in Christ', by which Christ is described as determining circumstance which conditions the life of the believer. Thus, justification takes place 'in Christ' (Gal. 2:7); the individual Christian is 'a man in Christ' (2 Cor. 12:2), and the churches are 'in Christ' (Gal, 1:22); Christian witness takes place 'in Christ' (1 Cor. 4:15; Phil. 1:13; 2 Cor. 2:17).[341]

3.4.1.2 "Messiah... God Blessed" (Rom 9:5)

Paul calls Christ as God in Rom 9:5 that demonstrating the extent to which Paul's experience of the risen Lord had caused him to qualify or transform his Jewish monotheism. This means that Paul had a high Christology even before he used the Christ Hymn in Philippians 2.[342]

3.4.1.3 "Who being in the Form of God..."

We can observe in Philippians 2:6-7 that Paul saw Jesus as having pre-cxistence and equality with God but that in his pre-existence he did not take advantage of all the prerogatives of deity. Thus, it seems likely that Paul here means two things: one is Jesus emptied himself of the prerogatives and glory of being divine or of the right to claim such prerogatives, these prerogatives would entail glory and lordship, which belonged to Christ by virtue of

340 Hawthrone, *Dictionary of Paul and His Letters*, 105.

341 Christopher Tucker, "*Christology and the New Testament Jesus and his Earliest Followers*" (Edinburgh: University Press, 2001), 40-69.

342 David K. Lowery, "A Theology of Paul's Missionary Epistles" in *A Biblical Theology of the New Testament,* edited by Roy B. Zuck (Chicago: Moody Press, 1994), 255.

his being equal with God. Second is he poured himself out, rather than telling us what he gave up?[343]

In the New Testament this title is routinely given to Jesus as the Provider of salvation e.g., Paul applied Joel 2:32 to Jesus in Rom. 10:13, "Everyone who calls on the name of the Lord shall be saved". The confession "Jesus is Lord" is used by Paul as a summary statement faith for those saved (Rom. 10:9). Similarly when he told the Corinthians that "no one can say, 'Jesus is Lord,' except by the Holy Spirit" (1Cor 12:3), he was not denying the possibility of false profession.[344] Rather, he was affirming the role of the Spirit in bringing people to a confession that epitomized their faith.

Also associated with the idea of Jesus as Lord, is recognition of his authority over people. When Paul, for example, advised Christians about how wisely to handle various debatable issues of personal conviction and behavior (Rom 14-15), he reminded his readers that in the final analysis the only one to whom they were accountable in these matters was the Lord (Rom 14:8b-9).[345]

The majority of Paul's uses of 'Lord' for Jesus relate to the present or to the future. Rarely does Paul look to the past and speak of Jesus as Lord: as already noted he does not speak of 'the Lord dying' or 'the crucified Lord.'[346] He does, however, frequently refer to Jesus' coming in the future in terms of Jesus as Lord: for example, in 1 Thessalonians 4:13-18, Jesus is referred to as 'Lord' five times in quick succession; and in 1 Corinthians 16:22 the Aramaic *Maranatha* invocation is used by Paul to pray for the Lord (= Jesus) to come.[347]

343 I.H. Marshal, "Titles of Jesus Christ" in *New Bible Dictionary,* edited by I.H. Marshal et, al. (Secunderabad: OM Books, 3rd ed., 2000), 581.

344 Hawthrone, *Dictionary of Paul and His Letters*, 106.

345 Hawthrone, *Dictionary of Paul and His Letters*, 107.

346 Marshal, "Titles of Jesus Christ"..., 580-581.

347 David K. Lowery, "A Theology of Paul's Missionary Epistles" in *A Biblical Theology of the New Testament,* edited by Roy B. Zuck (Chicago: Moody Press, 1994), 253-256.

3.4.1.4 Christ and the Spirit

It has been noted often how closely Paul identifies Christ and the Spirit in his letters- indeed, at points they seem to be identical. Paul can speak of the Spirit coming to believers only because Christ is risen and ascended. For example, in discussing Jesus' resurrection, Paul speaks of Jesus, the last Adam, as a "life giving Spirit" (1Cor 15:45).[348] Thus, in the church age Christ and spirit are not one but two in identity, but they are one in function because the Spirit is Christ's agent on earth. Paul knows no doctrine of second baptism, for by the Spirit one enters Christ's body, and that is the only occasion which Paul speaks of as being baptized by the Spirit (1Cor 12: 13).[349]

3.4.2 The Humanity of the Christ

3.4.2.1 Christ as Son

It seems that Paul understood Jesus as human also apart from as divine, but did not spell out in any detail how he defined that humanity. This may be because of the facts of Jesus and his ministry was assumed knowledge on the part of Paul and his readers. It may also reflect Paul's chosen emphasis in his letters on Jesus' death and resurrection, and issues of life in the Spirit and in the church. Furthermore, the eschatological events of first importance for Paul seems to have been Christ's taking on true human nature and humbling himself to the status of a servant, his death on the cross and his resurrection.[350]

As in the Gospels, the expression "Son of God" primarily identifies Jesus' role as the Representative of God who faithfully carries out His will. But in contrast to the Gospels, Paul, for example, said that Jesus was "declared with power to be the Son

348 Christopher Tucker, "*Christology and the New Testament Jesus and his Earliest Followers*" (Edinburgh: University Press, 2001), 56-60.

349 Tucker, "*Christology and the New Testament*..., 56-60.

350 Tucker, "*Christology and the New Testament*..., 56-60.

of God by his resurrection from the dead: Jesus Christ our Lord" (Rom. 1:4).[351]

Secondly Paul, in 1 Thessalonians 1:10, exhorts his readers 'to wait for his Son from heaven, whom he raised from the dead-Jesus, who rescues us from the wrath that is coming.' Jesus *qua* Son seems to be primarily the one who is to come at the *parousia*. 1 Corinthians 15:28 also looks forward to the End-time and refers to Jesus as Son; but there the 'activity' of Jesus *qua* Son is not to be coming in any salvific role, but finally and definitively submitting himself to the power and authority of God.[352]

3.4.2.2 Last Adam

Paul uses the Adam typology of Jesus and in 1Cor 15:45 calls Jesus the Last Adam. Rom 5:12-18; 1 Tim 2:5; 1Cor 15:21-23, 44-49 Rom 6:3-4 are evidences where Paul presents and deals with the Last Adam typology comparing with Jesus as the Last Adam in whom all who believed would be saved.

The point is simply stated: in and by the resurrection, Christ became "last Adam." As we saw the theological logic of Adam Christology could be extended back to include Jesus' whole life. But the focus of Adam Christology lies clearly in Christ's death and resurrection. And if the exposition of the theme in Romans 5 centers on the death of Christ (5.15-19),[353] the exposition of 1 Corinthians 15 certainly centers on the resurrection of Christ. As Adam stands for death, so Christ a stands for resurrection-1Cor 15.21-22:

> 21 For since death came through a human being, the resurrection of the dead has come also through a human being. 22 For as in Adam all die, so also in Christ shall all be made alive?[354]

351 Hawthrone, *Dictionary of Paul and His Letters*, 109.

352 Hawthrone, *Dictionary of Paul and His Letters*, 109.

353 Hawthrone, *Dictionary of Paul and His Letters*, 109.

354 Lowery, "A Theology of Paul's Missionary Epistles"..., 253-256.

In this case we could combine thought of death and resurrection without strain: as Adam represents humankind through life to death, so Christ represents humankind through death to life. Similarly with the use of Ps 8:4-6 in the further Adam Christology of 15:27: God "has subjected everything under his feet" (Ps 8:6). Although an allusion to Ps 8:4-5 may also be implied in reference to Christ's life (as in Heb 2:6-9),[355] the thought in 1Cor 15:27 is exclusively on the exaltation of the resurrected Christ. It is the risen and exalted Christ who fulfills and completes the divine plan for humankind. Most striking of all is Paul's third recourse to Adam Christology within the same chapter-1Cor 15:44-45.

> 44If there is a natural body; there is also a spiritual body.
> 45 Thus, also it is written: "the first man Adam became a living soul;" the last Adam [became] life-giving spirit.[356]

Adam represents the former; the race of humanity which ends in death, the embodiment which cannot make the transition through death without transformation. Christ represents the final; the race of humanity which begins from the resurrection of the dead, the embodiment of resurrection.[357] The first Adam stands for humankind from creation up to death. The last Adam stands for eschatological humankind, the life of the new creation, from resurrection onwards (Gen 2.7; 1Cor 15:45). However, he did compare and contrast Christ and Adam at different times in Romans and 1 Corinthians. When he described Christ as "the last Adam" in Corinthians, the adjective "last" underscores the difference between the two men.[358]

Paul viewed Adam as the one whose act of disobedience brought sin and death to all people (Rom 5:12; 1Cor 15:21-22). The obedience of Christ, on the other hand, brought life and the

---

355 Also Rom. 8.3 and Gal. 4.4-5.

356 NRSV.

357 Note how the Adam Christology of Heb. 2.6-9 is expounded in terms of Jesus' suffering as both representative and as "pioneer" leading many sons to glory through death to liberty (2.9-15).

358 NRSV.

promise of resurrection and eternal life to all those associated with Him (Rom 5:17; 1Cor 15:21-22). The existence embodied by the resurrected Christ is one where death has expended its sting and is now stingless (1Cor. 15.54-57).[359]

3.5 The Significance of the Resurrection

Paul considers the historical appearances of the risen Christ to be essential as an introduction to his general discussion of the resurrection theme in 1 Corinthians 15. The resurrection stands at the center of Paul's Christology as well as at the center of his experience.[360] The apostle recognizes that the list of appearances authenticates the fact of the resurrection, and he includes it as a preface to the mention of his own Damascus road experience.

For Paul, Christ's resurrection was God's affirmation that Jesus' death did indeed pay the penalty for sin (1Cor 15:17). This same point was made succinctly when he said that Christ "was delivered over to death for our sins and was raised to life for our justification" (Rom 4:25). The resurrection testified to the fact that Jesus' death made possible acquittal from sin's penalty, escape from sin's power, and ultimate deliverance from sin's presence. Jesus' resurrection also initiated His role as Lord. He now exercises authority at God's right hand. Paul referred to this when he said that Jesus "was declared with power to be the Son of God by his resurrection from the dead: Jesus Christ our Lord (1:4).

The resurrection is then not so much a work that Christ did as it is a work of God the Father and the Spirit. Yet Paul regarded the resurrection as integrally related to Jesus' present ministry and an essential aspect of Christian's future experience.[361]

359 Lowery, "A Theology of Paul's Missionary Epistles"..., 253-256.

360 Lowery, "A Theology of Paul's Missionary Epistles"..., 253-256.

361 James D. G. Dunn, *Theology of Paul the Apostle* (Michigan: William B. Eerdmans Publishing Company, 1998), 242.

3.6 Christ as the Image of God

Paul also describes Jesus Christ as "the image of God" (2Cor 4:4; Col 1:15; cf. Rom 8:29). Such a formulation hearkens back to Genesis 1:27, where Adam (and Eve) is made "according to the image of God" *(κατ' εί κό να θεοῦ)*. We often think of an image as an imperfect or lifeless copy of the original, but Paul understands the image to partake of the reality and the nature of the original. The special role which Christ has in salvation as the image of God is the role which he played in creation (Col 1:15-20).[362] Human beings born in Adam would never bring about a world of joy and goodness since they too have sinned (Rom 5:12-19). Jesus the Messiah, however, succeeded where Adam failed. Through him God's plan to bring the world under his lordship will succeed.

Paul does not only identify Jesus as the second Adam, nor does he equate Adam and Jesus in every respect. Adam was created "according to the image of God" (Gen 1:27), but Jesus "is the image of God" (2Cor 4:4; Col 1:15). Christ as the image of God surpasses Adam because the word image suggests that he shares the very nature of God. Jesus is not only the second Adam; he is also the agent of creation and the goal of creation (Col 1:16).[363]

Only through Jesus Christ, the one and only image of God, can human beings attain what God intended in making Adam according to his image (2Cor 3:18; Eph 4:24). Indeed, those who are "conformed to the image of his Son" (Rom 8:29) are predestined by God to share in this joy.[364] He is not image in the sense of a reproduction or likeness, but in the sense of essence. Therefore, we can know who God is by knowing Christ.[365]

---

362 Donald Guthrie, *New Testament Theology* (Illinois, Leicester: InterVarsity Press, 1981), 385-386.

363 Lowery, "A Theology of Paul's Missionary Epistles"..., 273.

364 Pheme Perkins, *New Testament Introduction* (Allahabad: ST Pauls, 2002), 249.

365 Perkins, *New Testament Introduction*..., 249-250.

3.7 Paul's Christology in His Thought World

3.7.1 Eschatology

Pauline understanding on eschatology set a frame work for many other important topics such as Christology, pneumatology, ecclesiology and anthropology are all built upon the eschatological foundation of Paul's thought. Paul's eschatological outlook was surely transformed once he became a follower of Jesus. Paul interrelates Christological and eschatological aspects together because both have similar types of connotation for the believers.[366]

3.7.2 The Meaning of Eschatology and Jewish Understanding

The word 'eschatology' refers to the study of last things. It is derived from the Greek word ἔσχατος meaning "last" or "Final" in the spatial or material temporary existence.[367] It includes studies such as, "the future of the world, the *parousia* of Jesus Christ, the coming kingdom of God, the last judgment of humankind, the resurrection from the dead, heaven and hell, the transformation of the cosmos."[368] However, during the recent years a second meaning of eschatology has been developed, that the messiah who supposed to come at the end of time will come again. For what God has done in Christ is parallel to what the Jews expected God to do in the future.[369]

To understand Paul's eschatology one must be aware of the history of Israel's eschatological expectation as eschatological expectation was an integral part of Israel's faith.[370] The Jewish understanding presents that God who is the one and only God who

366 Thomas R. Schreiner, *Paul* (Leicester: InterVarsity Press, 2001), 155-156.

367 Joe Blair, *Introducing the New Testament* (Nashville, Tennessee: Broadmen and Holman Publishers, 1994), 162.

368 Hawthrone, *Dictionary of Paul and His Letters*, 112.

369 Gerhard Kittel and Gerhard Friedrich, *Theological Dictionary of the New Testament*, abridged in one volume by Geoffrey W. Bromiley (Grand Rapids, Michigan: William B. Eerdmans Publishing Company, 1984), 264.

370 Gerald F. Hawthorne, Ralph P. Martin and Daniel G. Reid, eds., "Eschatology," *Dictionary of Paul and His Letters,* 253.

is capable of, and committed to, acting in the future to defeat their enemies and God's own people will be liberated through God's action.[371] Jewish people thought that God will be their Liberator and on due time God will be a Judge for all Nations; however, it is noticed that Jesus Christ was presented as a Messiah by the earliest Christian community but for Jewish Messiah still is awaited.

Moreover, Daniel 7: 9-10 provides a vivid illustration of God's judgment metered out against his enemies. We learn from 12:1-2 that this judgment is to take place following the resurrection of the dead. Once again, Daniel's revelation adds to and compliments the revelation of the other prophets. Following on chronologically in the process of the judgment that Daniel describes, "books" being opened (7:10) though the contents on these books is not mentioned. Chapter 12:1 refers to a book in which the names of the righteous are written. Very similar ideas are expressed very early in the Old Testament when the Lord refers to a book that only contains the names of the righteous (Exo 32:32-33; cf. Ps 69:28).

Isaiah mentions a record of those worthy of life in the age to come (4:3) and Mal 3:16 written at the very close to the OT revelatory periods speaks of a "book of remembrance that was written before him of those who revered the LORD and thought on his name. So, we can say that the theology of Daniel is marks a development rather than an innovation in the theological concepts he makes use of. Therefore, based on the traditions such as the patriarchal promise, Sinai covenant and the David-Zion tradition the concept of eschatology has been observed that is very significant in the context of New Testament and Pauline corpus.[372] This eschatological theology continued even in the inter-testament period because they were convinced that the end was near and ordered their beliefs and communal practices accordingly.

---

371 D.E.H. Whiteley, *The Theology of Paul* (Great Britain: Basil Blackwell, 1972), 233.

372 H.J. Schoeps, *Paul: The Theology of the Apostle in the Light of Jewish Religious History*, translated by Harold Knight (Philadelphia: The Westminster Press, 1961), 88-89.

3.7.3 Eschatology in Pauline Corpus

In Pauline letters we read that Early Christians were waiting for the second coming as Jesus himself promised (Jn 14:18-19), but When Christ delayed and did not come "yet," questions arose, and even doubts, until Paul was obliged to explain the "second coming status" to the church of Thessalonica. Paul's two letters to the Thessalonians are among the earliest writings of the NT.[373]

Eschatological aspect is considered as an essential part of Paul's thoughts and formulation. The concept of the future drives his hopes, passion and mission. Therefore his eschatology is the one area one should began with in Pauline study.[374] The framework of Paul's entire theological thought is that of apocalyptic dualism of *This Age* and the *Age to come*. For Paul the redemptive blessings brought to human by Jesus' death and resurrection and the giving of the Holy Spirit are eschatological events. Because of these eschatological events, the believer lives a life called the New Age. The very phrase describing the status of the believers, '*in Christ*,' is an eschatological term. To be '*in Christ*' means to be in the *New Age*, '*For if any man is in Christ he/she is a new creation; old things had passed away and new things has come*.' (II Cor 5:17).[375]

Pauline understanding on eschatology set a framework for many other important themes such as Christology, pneumatology, ecclesiology, soteriology and anthropology are all built upon the eschatological foundation of Paul's thought. Every letter within the Pauline corpus presents and provides eschatological concerns. To know more about eschatology it is significant to understand the terminologies that Paul himself used in the context of eschatological development.

---

373 N.T. Wright, *Paul: In Fresh Perspective* (Minneapolis: Fortress Press, 205), 131.

374 David L. Peterson, "Eschatology," in *The Anchor Bible Dictionary,* edited by David Noel Freedman et al., Vol. 2 (New York: Double Day, 1992), 576.

375 S. Sobanaraj, *Diversity in Paul's Eschatology: Paul's View on the Parousia and Bodily Resurrection* (Delhi: ISPCK, 2007), 135.

3.7.3.1 Παρουσία

In the epistles to the Thessalonians the Second Coming is called παρουσία '*Parousia*' which means, active presence, coming, advent. In Greek literature this word is generally used for the solemn visit of an emperor, king, or some great personage. It is therefore aptly used for the day of the Lord, the triumphal return of Christ, which would denote the end of history.[376] Paul uses it frequently in the Thessalonians epistles (1Thess. 2:19; 3:13; 4:15; 5:23 & 2 Thess. 2:1; 8-9, and 1 15:23) to indicate both immediate and extended expectation of the second coming of Christ.[377] It signifies that the second coming of Christ would be an event different in character from the incarnation one. Gradually the word came to be distinctly used to denote an event in the future, which would witness the second coming of Christ.[378]

3.7.3.2 Ἀποκάλυψις (Revelation, Declaration)

Paul also uses this word to refer to the second coming of the Lord. The word "apocalypse" means an "unveiling" or "disclosure." The power and glory that are reveal to the world. Christ has already been, by his resurrection and exaltation, to the right hand of God where he has been given sovereignty over all spiritual foes (1 cor. 15:25).[379]

The word is also used for Christ coming in Glory (II thess.1:7 "at the revelation of our Lord Jesus Christ from Heaven" cf. 1 Cor.1:7 "waiting for the revelation of our Lord Jesus Christ from heaven").[380]

---

376 Irving F Wood, "Paul's Eschatology," *JSTOE: The Biblical World* 38/2 (August 1911): 79-91.

377 George Eldon Ladd, *A Theology of the New Testament* (Michigan: William B. Eerdmans Publishing Company, 1974), pp. 550-551.

378 N.T. Wright, *Paul: In Fresh Perspective*, 142.

379 Gerald F. Hawthorne, Ralph P. Martin and Daniel G. Reid, eds., "Eschatology," *Dictionary of Paul and His Letters*, 259; Gerhard Kittel and Gerhard Friedrich, *Theological Dictionary of the New Testament*, 793.

380 Gopal Ghorai, "Pauline Eschatology," *2 Miles* (May, 2010).

3.7.3.3 Ἐπιφάνεια (Appearance)

The word is used with reference to the appearance of the Lord Jesus Christ in 2Thess. 2:8. The return of the lord will be no secret, hidden event but a breaking into history of the glory of God. God has already broken the power of death and displayed the reality of life and immortality with in history through the appearing of our saviour Christ Jesus in the flesh (1 Tim.1:10).[381]

3.7.3.4 Eschatologia (End of Times)

It is a special expression for the description of the end of the world and times. Paul gave a Christian dimension to it. Realizing that the end of times does not mean only the end of the world, but the beginning of the realization of God's will in Jesus Christ. Through his incarnation, death, resurrection, ascension, descent of the Holy Spirit on the believers: all these events together are signs for the end of times preparing for the final and last event to happen that is the second coming (2Thess. 1:7; 1Cor. 1:7, Acts 1:10-11).[382]

3.7.3.5 Ἡμέρα (Day)

It is the "Day of Yahweh" in the OT, it is an expression used by the prophets to describe God's wrath and judgment (Am 5:18; Iss 2:12-22), the eternal kingdom for the good ones, and the judgment for the evil ones (Zec 14:11-15; Joel 3:14-21). So, when talks about the "day of Christ Jesus" (Phil 1:10; 2:16), it is the same as with "the day of the Lord," which the Paul uses in 1Thess 5:2, 1Cor 1:8, 5:5 and 2Cor 1:14. The Old Testament uses it in relation to day of Yahweh's, however for Paul it is referred to the meeting with the exalted Christ (1Thess 1:10). So, the "day of Christ Jesus" is without any doubt the eschatological of Christian life.[383]

---

381 G.E. Ladd, *Theology of the New Testament* (Grand Rapids: William B. Eerdmans Publishing Company, 1974), 555.

382 H. Ridderbos, *Paul: The Outline of His Theology* (Grand Rapids: William B. Eerdmans Publishing Company, 1975), 529.

383 G.E. Ladd, *Theology of the New Testament*..., 555.

However, the following aspects[384] also help to understand the eschatology in Pauline corpus:

- The sleep of dead
- The return of Christ
- The kingdom of God
- The mystery of Lawlessness
- The mystery of Israel's hardening and final salvation
- The resurrection and rapture
- The judgment
- The consummation

3.7.4 Paul on Resurrection

The Corinthians had difficulty accepting the idea of bodily resurrection. If Paul had taught of immortality of the soul or the resurrection of the spirit into the realm of God the Corinthians would have had no problem. In 1 Corinthians 15:20 and 15:23 he describes the risen Lord Jesus Christ as the first fruits (ἀπαρχὴ), implying that the believer will share in the resurrection life in the same way that the full harvest is related to the initial crop. So, Paul associates the resurrection of the saints with the resurrection of Christ that the same power that raised Christ will raise up his people (1Cor 6:14; II cor. 4:14). However Paul had no word to the resurrection of those who do not stand in solidarity with Christ.[385] And without the resurrection, there is no new life in this world because evil is still in control. The lack of reference to a resurrection of non-Christian does not prove that Paul denied its possibility, but it does indicate that Paul's primary concern is the future if believers.[386]

384 Gerald F. Hawthorne, Ralph P. Martin and Daniel G. Reid, eds., "Eschatology," *Dictionary of Paul and His Letters*, 260-261.

385 Heinz Giesen, "Eschatology in Philippians," in *Paul and His Theology,* edited by Stanley E. Porter (Leiden, Boston: Brill, 2006), 224-225.

386 G.E. Ladd, *Theology of the New Testament...*, 550-568.

3.7.5 Paul on Judgment of God

Paul takes over the Jewish expectation of God's Judgment that all men and women will be held accountable before God for their lives. In I Corinthians 3:12-15, Paul offers an extended passage about the final judgment of God using the metaphor of a building materials being tested by the purifying fires of "the Day." And in Romans 2:16 God is said to judge the secrets of humankind by Christ Jesus. It is not only the humankind of lawlessness who will be judged but it is also the ultimate judgment and defeat of Satan along with his angelic minions.[387]

Paul did not envisage believers as exempt from that *final judgment*. This image affirms moral significance for human actions. Believers should not make the mistake for which Paul criticizes Israel (Romans 2) by thinking that because they are in process of "being saved" they will therefore be exempt from the moral consequences of their actions. The gracious God is also the impartial Judge. This point is made clear in 1 Cor. 3.10-15.[388]

3.7.6 Paul on the Wrath of God

The word "wrath" when applied to God carries with it the notion of judgment. In Rom. 1:18, the righteousness and wrath are placed side by side.[389] The wrath of God expresses itself against all sin. In Rom. 2:1-11, Paul expounds this judgment to them, but maintaining that wrath and fury are reserved for those who obey wickedness and do not obey truth.

3.7.7 Albert Schweitzer Views on Eschatology

Albert Schweitzer was born in the Alsatian in 1875. His father, Ludwig Schweitzer, was a Lutheran pastor. A number of his ancestors on both sides were pastors and organists. So, it is not

---

387 G.E. Ladd, *Theology of the New Testament,* 564.

388 Henry M. Shires, *The Eschatology of Paul: In the Light of Modern Scholarship* (Philadelphia: The Westminster Press, 1946), 77-83.

389 Gerald F. Hawthorne, Ralph P. Martin and Daniel G. Reid, eds. "Eschatology," *Dictionary of Paul and His Letters*, 261-262.

much of a surprise that in 1893 he began to study theology in Strasbourg. He became one of the most influential contributors to the study of the historical Jesus and the theology of the apostle Paul in the 20th century. However, among the wider public he is probably better remembered as missionary doctor in Lambaréné and as winner of the Nobel Peace Prize.

A very brief review of his theological work in chronological order will help to reconstruct his development of thought. After Schweitzer had finished his first theological study in 1898 he did his doctoral in philosophy in Strasbourg a year later. His dissertation dealt with Kant's philosophy of religion and was published also in 1899. A second theological exam and the licentiate degree followed in the year 1900. For the latter Schweitzer wrote a dissertation on the Lord's Supper. As a second part to this he soon added a "sketch" on the messianic secret and the life of Jesus and his suffering. In 1901, by the age of 26, Schweitzer had already published three dissertations and became *Privatdozent*[390] in the Protestant Theological Faculty in Strasbourg a year later.

The first edition of his opus magnum *Von Reimarus zu Wrede* (*The Quest of the Historical Jesus*) was published in 1906 Schweitzer demonstrated how all the modern historical reconstructions of the life of Jesus simply attributed to Jesus in the liberal theology. He held that Jesus believed the apocalyptic kingdom of God would momentarily appear, in response to the zealous piety of himself and his disciples. Thus, Jesus taught an '*interim ethic*' the need for absolute righteousness, if one hoped to enter the kingdom. Jesus' values of higher righteousness, love and faith called for extreme application because of the extremity of the times.[391] It grew out of the earlier "sketch" and his lectures on life-of-Jesus research during the summer semester 1905. Schweitzer himself dates the first draft of *The Mysticism of Paul the Apostle*

390 Gerald F. Hawthorne, Ralph P. Martin and Daniel G. Reid, eds., "Eschatology," *Dictionary of Paul and His Letters*, 259.

391 Gerald F. Hawthorne, Ralph P. Martin and Daniel G. Reid, eds., "Eschatology," *Dictionary of Paul and His Letters*, 262.

to the year 1906. As an introduction to this study he reviewed the history of research in a similar fashion that he had already employed for *The Quest.*[392]

Albert Schweitzer was the first of the great attempts in biblical scholarship to understand the thought of the New Testament from the eschatological point of view. He propounded the word "consistent eschatology" is also sometimes known as apocalyptic eschatology.[393] He asserts that Jesus and his immediate followers were in an enthusiastic state of intense eschatological expectation and that the main theme of Jesus' preaching was the imminent end of the world. Anticipating the last judgment, Jesus preached repentance, that is, a life lived in expectation of the new age. Jesus goes even to death, in order to bring great changes in the world. He develops his idea further in his book, '*The mysticism of the Apostle Paul.*' In this he argues that, Paul holds on to the eschatological, saving significance of Jesus death in spite of the contrary course of history.

Paul interprets the proclaimed resurrection of Jesus as an emergent breaking in of the New Age into the old. According to him, the solution is to find the teaching of Jesus a certain '*spiritual force*' which he calls the '*religion of love*' and which can remain essentially the same in connection with varying world view. Paul like Jesus was influenced by the Jewish eschatological expectation and his thoughts run in this line throughout his eschatological development.[394] The kind of eschatology which Schweitzer finds is futuristic, apocalyptic and world denying. He points out that the eschatology of John the Baptist, Jesus, and Paul cannot be simply disposed of as a pitiable attempt to compensate for adverse time

---

392 Academic title conferred to one who denotes the ability to teach independently at University level without holding a professional chair.

393 R. M. Prince, 'Schweitzer Albert' in *New Dictionary Theology*, edited by Sinclair B. Ferguson and David F. Wright (Leicester: InterVarsity Press, 1988), 664-665.

394 "Albert Schweitzer's Understanding of Righteousness by Faith according to Paul's Letter to the Romans," SBL Annual Meeting 2007 in San Diego.

but rather this wave of apocalyptic enthusiasm was called forth solely by the appearance of the two great personalities.

He singles out Paul for special attention as he is the link to understand the dogma from Jesus to the later Greek theology and Schweitzer sees that Jesus and Paul share the same eschatological worldview and that Paul from his first letter to the last was uniformly dominated by the expectation of the immediate return of Jesus, of the judgment and the messianic glory and says that it is to take place at the End is not of purely spiritual redemption but that body and soul are redeemed together and that it is not only the elected part of human kind but the whole world is completely transformed in this event.[395] So, Schweitzer says of the Pauline eschatology as "a synthesis of the eschatology of the Prophets and the Son of Man Eschatology of Daniel."[396]

For Schweitzer, Paul's mysticism is not a God-Contact-Mysticism, but a Christ-Mediation-Mysticism, in which man cannot achieve a union with God directly, but may enter into a union with Christ, who is both man and God. And this contact is made by a literal co-experiencing of Christ's death and resurrection.[397] He stressed that Christ; the Son of God is the final revelation and everyone who believe in him will not be put to shame, which is also Paul's appeal to the Romans (Rom 10:11). The Son of Man is identified as the exalted Jesus with the eschatological Son of Man, thus most of the primitive Christology is a Son of Man Christology. The early Church awaited the coming of Jesus as the Son of Man.[398]

Paul's mysticism goes back to the dying and rising of Christ, which took place in the immediate past and in the death of Jesus began the cessation of the natural world and in his resurrection

395 Neill Q. Hamilton, *The Holy Spirit and Eschatology in Paul* (London: Oliver and Boyd Ltd, 1957), 41.

396 S. Sobanaraj, *Diversity in Paul's Eschatology: Paul's view on the Parousia and Bodily Resurrection,* 33.

397 Neill Hamilton, *The Holy Spirit and Eschatology in Paul*, 42-46.

398 Albert Schweitzer, *The Mysticism of Paul the Apostle* (New York: The Macmillan Co., 1955), 76.

the dawning of the supernatural world. For Schweitzer, the prime importance of this dying and rising again is to put the believer in a position of advantage over other men. He claims that Paul held to two resurrections, a messianic and a general and to two corresponding blessedness, a temporary and an eternal.[399]

Schweitzer treated the delay of *parousia* as endangering the faith of the early church and that justification by faith as a starting point would lead to a misunderstanding of Paul, and that this doctrine was only a side issue. He finds the real clue to understanding Paul's thought and experience in union with Christ rather than in justification. The center of Pauline thought is the realization of the coming new age of the redemption by the work of Christ. In this regard Schweitzer also pointed that there is a danger in making justification by faith the central doctrine, depriving Paul's message of its '*redemptive historical dynamic*' and making it into a timeless treatment of individual justification.[400]

3.7.8 Eschatology as a Vital Foundation

According to Paul, the death and resurrection of Christ is an eschatological event which "tossed the foundation of the new creation" (2Cor 5:17, cf. Is 43, 65, 66).[401] Paul understood Christ-event as escorting in a new age, even the last days. What has been foretold to happen in the future has come true in Christ? Jesus of Nazareth is without doubt the Messiah, the Christ promised of the Old Testament who descended from the line of David according to the flesh and declared son of God as from the resurrection of the death (Rom 1:4 speaks of Jesus resurrection as "the resurrection of the death" rather than his resurrection from the death).[402] And Paul in 1Cor 15:20-23 sees Jesus resurrection as "the first fruits"

399 Albert Schweitzer, "The Mysticism of Paul," http://www.apocryphile.org/jrm/articles/paul.html

400 G. E. Ladd, *A Theology of the New Testament*, 337.

401 Albert Schweitzer, "The Mysticism of Paul," 46-47.

402 G. E. Ladd, *A Theology of the New Testament,* 373-374.

of the general resurrection. This salvific work of Christ marked a decisive beginning of a new epoch.[403]

Paul's encounter with the risen Christ disrupted the previous schema, for Christ's coming and resurrection were perceived as the eschatological climax – "the fullness of time" (Gal 4:4), the beginning of "the resurrection of the death" (Rom. 1:4). But the end did not come: the dead were not raised; the judgment did not take place. The eschatological climax was thus incomplete; the completion of the divine purpose required a further climactic act. Christ, who had already come, must come again, only then, the rest of the final events would unfold.

This disruption required Paul to modify his eschatological schema because the single division of the time line, dividing present age from age to come, had itself been split into a two stage division making the two ages overlap with each other. Hence, Paul articulates this overlapping of the two ages in terms of the believers already being saved but one which awaits a final consummation what is commonly called as the "already and not-yet."[404]

3.7.8.1 The Eschatological Tautness that leads towards the Concept of "Already but Not Yet"

The distinctive feature of Paul's theology at this point is not the eschatology but the tension which his revised eschatology sets up. Eschatological hope was a common feature of Paul's religious heritage. But an eschatology split in this way between such a decisive "already" and yet still a "not yet" was a new departure. It follows that the weight of Paul's eschatology is not forward-looking but backward looking, or at least lies in the tension between the two.

Paul's theology is eschatological not because of what he still hoped would happen, but because of what he believed had already

403 G.K. Beale, "Eschatology" in *Dictionary of the Later New Testament and its Development,* edited by Ralph Martin and Peter David (Leicester: InterVarsity Press,1997), 331.

404 Gerald F. Hawthorne, Ralph P. Martin and Daniel G. Reid, eds., "Eschatology," *Dictionary of Paul and His Letters*, 256-258.

happened. What had already happened (Easter and Pentecost) had already the character of the end and showed what the end would be like. Which also means that the character of the interim period as "eschatological" did not depend on the *parousia* alone, nor to any real extent on either the imminence or delay of the *parousia.* What mattered was the fact that "the powers of the age to come" (Heb. 6.5) were already shaping lives and communities, as they would also in due course shape the cosmos.[405]

This means that the believers live in the overlap of the ages, "between the times." Believers are "in Adam" and continue to be "in Adam" but they are also "in Christ," and have begun to experience life, though they have yet to share the full experience of Christ's resurrection. Fundamental to Paul's conception of the process of salvation, therefore, is his conviction that the believers has not yet arrived, is not yet perfect. But the eschatological hope of Paul is that, just as the believers share in the suffering of Christ in the present age afflictions, they will also be raised like Christ in the resurrection of the body.[406]

3.7.9 Eschatological Contribution: Albert Schweitzer Views and Understanding

First, it is bold enough to take seriously the apocalyptic passages in the world of and in the recorded words of Jesus. This is not to say that Schweitzer was right in taking these passages as the dominant note in the message of Jesus. Yet it is too easy a way out of the dilemma to dismiss them all as first century interpolations.[407]

A second contribution lies in the fact that Schweitzer never renounced his allegiance to Jesus or his sense of the validity of the call of Jesus to the service of human need. Jesus was certainly wrong in his expectation of an imminent and cataclysmic end of

405 Gerald F. Hawthorne, Ralph P. Martin and Daniel G. Reid, eds., "Eschatology," *Dictionary of Paul and His Letters*, 258.

406 Gerald F. Hawthorne, Ralph P. Martin and Daniel G. Reid, eds., "Eschatology," *Dictionary of Paul and His Letters*, 254-255.

407 James D.G. Dunn, *Theology of Paul the Apostle* (Grand Rapids: William B. Eerdmans Publishing Company, 1998), 464-465.

the present world and coming of the kingdom, yet he still remains our Lord who calls us to be his followers[408] and Christ is not the end but the beginning of understanding future.

A third contribution comes out more clearly in Schweitzer's other major work among the considerable number he wrote, *The Mysticism of Paul the Apostle.* There he maintains that Paul's conception of the kingdom, though he expected an imminent end of the world, was far from other-worldly in its bearing on the Christian life. The kingdom is not a human achievement, nor is it wholly a matter of personal piety. It is God's kingly rule to become manifest in the human scene through divine irruption from beyond it, and thus, we await with faith and hope its consummation. "To be a Christian means to be possessed and dominated by a hope of the Kingdom of God."[409]

Schweitzer's apocalyptic interpretations of Jesus are open to challenge. Perhaps the shortcoming most commonly pointed out is that he did not take seriously enough in his analysis the ethical teachings of Jesus in relation to the message of the kingdom. It has been charged that he formulated his apocalyptic position at the beginning of his study and then without full objectivity shaped his textual conclusions around it by regarding as authentic the passages which corroborate it.[410]

3.8. Soteriology

Paul's Christology changed the shape of his soteriology. Unless new finds from the Qumran scrolls change matters, there is no conclusive evidence that early Jews were expecting a crucified Messiah it was the story of death and resurrection of Jesus that caused Paul to rethink how salvation would be accomplished.

---

408 James D.G. Dunn, *Theology of Paul the Apostle*, 467-468.

409 Georgia Harkness, "Understanding the Kingdom of God," http://www.religion-online.org/showchapter.asp?title=577&C=738

410 Georgia Harkness, "Understanding the Kingdom of God," http://www.religion-online.org/showchapter.asp?title=577&C=738

3.8.1 Colossians 1:15-20

Colossians 1:15-20 is one of the most significant texts in the whole New Testament, describing the divinity of Jesus Christ with great precision and fullness. Lightfoot rightly gets the gist of the passage, commenting on verse 18:

> And not only does He hold this position of absolute priority and sovereignty over the Universe – the natural creation. He stands also in the same relation to the Church – the new spiritual creation. He is its head, and it is His body. This is His prerogative, because He is the source and the beginning of its life, being the First-born from the dead. Thus, in all things – in the spiritual order as in the natural – in the Church as in the World – He is found to have the pre-eminence.[411]

This hymn talks about the God's power in Jesus Christ therefore, it has written to praise Jesus and his redemptive work.[412] The hymn focuses on creation and presents Jesus as son of God as the image of the invisible God. However, Philo and papyrus argued that wisdom is a reflection of eternal life, a spotless mirror of the working of God, and an image of His goodness.[413] Furthermore, it is clear that Christ is the firstborn of all creation. This hymn is an example of high Christology. Col 1: 15-20 is cause wonder; for that Moule argued that Christ is not only the creator of all things but also the goal or purpose toward which the created world is destined to move.[414] Ziesler; like Moule, says:

> On the face of it, the hymn proclaims the pre-existence of Christ. Who as a person was active in both creation

411 Albert Schweitzer, *The Mysticism of Paul the Apostle*, 384.

412 Norman Perrin, *the Kingdom of God in the Teaching of Jesus* (Philadelphia: The Westminster Press, 1963), 32-34.

413 J. B. Lightfoot, *Saint's Paul's Epistles to the Colossians and to Philemon* (Grand Rapids: Zondervan Publishing House, 1879), 156.

414 Charles H. Talbert, *Ephesians and Colossians* (Michigan: Baker Academic, 2007), 182-183.

> and redemption? Yet our knowledge of Wisdom language must make us cautious; it is possible that what is meant is that the same full presence and activity of God evident in Christ's resurrection and reconciling work was also present at creation, so that what is pre-existent is not Christ in person, but the power of God that came to be active in him.[415]

The quotation of Ziesler leads us to a probable conclusion that Moule and Ziesler have difficulty accepting the high Christology in 1:15-20 because they cannot imagine how it could have developed so soon after the time of the historical figure executed by the Romans.[416] However, unlike Ziesler and Moule, Marianne Meye Thompson says that this hymn outlines the relationship of Christ to God and to creation, underscoring the cosmic scope of God's work in Christ and this hymn plays a significant role in the development of Christological thought.[417]

3.8.2 Phil 2:6-11

Phil 2:6-11 has been explained Christologically in two principal ways, as a purely Adam/Christ typology like in Rom 5:12-21 and 1Cor 15:22,[418] and as an incarnation/exaltation Christology that presupposes Christ's deity.[419] While there are some similarities to Paul's contrast between existence in Adam and in Christ, in the flesh and in the Spirit,[420] the major thrust of this hymn is quite different. Even if J.B. Lightfoot's philosophical analogies may be questioned, his arguments and conclusion remain persuasive. The phrases, "in the form of God" and "the being equal with God"

415 Talbert, *Ephesians and Colossians*, 187.

416 Talbert, *Ephesians and Colossians*, 192.

417 Talbert, *Ephesians and Colossians*, 192.

418 Talbert, *Ephesians and Colossians*, 192.

419 Marianne Meye Thompson, *Colossians and Philemon* (Michigan: William B. Eerdmans Publishing Company, 2005), 32.

420 J.D.G. Dunn, *Christology in the Making* (Grand Rapids: William B. Eerdmans Publishing Company, 1996), 114-121.

must apply to the attributes of the Godhead" in the pre-incarnate Lord.[421]

The second half of the hymn (2:9-11) supports this view of the matter. It ascribes to the exalted Christ "the name that is above every name" and applies to him the obeisance due only to Yahweh (Isa 45:23) and the confession, "Every knee shall bow . . . and every tongue confesses that JESUS CHRIST IS YAHWEH to the glory of God the Father."[422] On an Adam/Christ typology this conclusion would yield only an adoptionist Christology, a man becoming God. This understanding of Jesus as a pre-existent divine figure is, as Martin Hengel has argued, the same Christology that Paul had preached in Philippi 50 CE, "and one is tempted to say that more happened [in Christology] in this period of less than two decades than in the whole of the next seven centuries."[423]

In 1Cor 8:6 also Paul, using a preformed tradition, distinguishes, in binitarian fashion, deity from deity in terms of "God the Father" and "Lord."[424] In this respect he stands in the Jewish tradition of what Aubrey Johnson called The One and the Many in the Israelite Conception of God. The "oneness" of God was no more Unitarian than the "oneness" of Adam and Eve (Gen 2:24).[425] Probably Unitarian monotheism was a development in rabbinic Judaism, apparently in reaction to Christianity. In 1Cor 8:6 and in other passages[426] the Apostle supplies us with the raw material that will later be refined and defined in the church's doctrine of the Trinity.

---

421 P.T. O'Brien, *the Epistle to the Philippians* (Grand Rapids: William B. Eerdmans Publishing Company, 1991), 186-271.

422 E.g. Rom 8:9-17; 12:2; 13:14; Eph 4:22-24; Col 3:1-3, 9-10, 12-4.

423 J.B. Lightfoot, *Saint Paul's Epistle to the Philippians* (Peabody, MA: Hendrickson, 1993), 127-133.

424 D.B. Capes, *Old Testament Yahweh Texts in Paul's Christology* (Tubingen: Mohr-Siebeck, 1992), 164-165, 167-70.

425 Martin Hengel, *The Son of God* (London: SCM, 1976), 1-2.

426 Elsewhere the contrast may be between God and Lord (1 Cor 12:5-6; 2 Cor 13:14) or between God the Father and Son (1 Cor 15:24-28).

3.9 Paul's Mission to Jews and Non-Jews: A Theological Debate

Paul's conversion also led him to perceive his Gentile mission as the divinely purpose (Gal 1:15). According to Udo Schnelle Paul experienced Damascus' incident as participation in the Christ event, which gave him a new identity and compelled him to restructure his picture of himself and the world. He further says that God granted Paul a new knowledge of the person of Jesus Christ and gave him a new assignment: to proclaim the gospel of Jesus Christ to the Gentiles.[427] To put it differently gentile mission is the outcome of Paul's conversion experience because that experience was in essence a conversion from Pharisaic Judaism to Messianic Judaism or from Torah to Christ. It was a conversion from Judaism to universal religion in which ethnic distinction between Jews and Gentiles were eradicated.[428]

However, whether Paul's call to the gentile mission really coincides with Christophany is a matter of debate. There are two views related to this: one is that Paul's Gentile mission originated during Damascus Road Experience; the other view is that it originated after the Damascus Road experience. Scholars like Seyoom Kim[429] and F.F. Bruce[430] see the Damascus Road Experience itself as the direct source and origin of Paul's new conviction about the Gentile.

Similarly, Krister Stendahl[431] claims that Paul perceived his Damascus Road Experience essentially as a call to be an apostle to the Gentile. On the other hand, a completely different idea about Paul's Gentile mission has been proposed by Francis Watson,

427 Ellis, *"God: Unity in Plurality," Old Testament* (n. 9), 112-16.

428 1 Cor 12:4-6; 2 Cor 13:14; Eph 4:4a, 5-6.

429 Udo Schnelle, *Apostle Paul: His Life and Theology* (Grand Rapids: Baker Academics, 2003), 101.

430 Terence Donaldson, *Paul and Gentiles: Remapping the Apostle's Convictional World* (Minneapolis: Fortress Press, 1997), 16.

431 Kim, *The Origin of Paul's Gospel*, 57. On the basis of Gal 1:16 he concludes that for Paul the Christophany on the Damascus Road Experience constituted both his gospel and his apostolic commission to the Gentile.

stating that Paul turned to the Gentiles in frustration after failing as a Christian missionary to his fellow Jews. Francis Watson further says that in order to ensure success of his mission among the Gentiles Paul discarded the normal legal requirements, which in turn separated Paul from Jewish community.[432]

E.P. Blair[433] also supports and agrees with the argument of Francis Watson. E.P. Blair see Gentile mission originated just before Paul's meeting with the Pillar apostles in Jerusalem. He argues that it was during this visit that Paul's temple vision narrated in Acts 22:17-21 occurred, which sealed his conviction regarding the Gentiles.[434] Therefore, both Francis Watson and E.P. Blair argue that Paul's Gentile mission originated after Damascus Experience. However, both the arguments do not take serious account of Paul's Damascus Road Experience which presents Paul's conversion experience accompanied with a call to be an apostle to the Gentiles.

Further, Donaldson rightly critiques Standahl's view by saying that any attempt reduces Paul's Damascus Road Experience to that of a simple call should be seen in the light of his reconfigured convictions about Christ, Torah, Israel and so on. He further says that to account for Paul's Gentile mission simply by saying that his Damascus Road Experience was a call, without analyzing his changed convictions about Christ, Israel and Torah is futile.[435] Unlike the prophetic calling of the Old Testament prophets like Isaiah and Jeremiah Paul's commission was not limited to the Jews. Paul understood this new Gentile mission as the climax of the conversion experience.

---

432 Bruce, Paul: Apostle of the Heart Set Free, 75. According to F.F. Bruce Paul's word in Gal 1:15ff indicate that he perceived call and commissioning were part of his conversion experience.

433 Krister Standahl, *Paul among Jews and Gentile* (Philadelphia: Fortress Press, 1976), 7-23.

434 Francis Watson, *Paul, Judaism and Gentiles: A Sociological Approach* (Cambridge: Cambridge University Press, 1986), 30-38.

435 E.P Blair, "Paul's Call to the Gentile Mission," *Biblical Research* 10 (1965): 19-33.

Luke presents at least three different views about Gentile mission:

a) *Mission to Gentiles replaces mission to Israel:* According to Jack T. Sanders Luke basically anti-Semitic and regards the Jewish rejection of the gospel as a typical for a people who have always rebelled against God (Acts 7: 51-53).[436]
b) *Mission to Gentiles supplements mission to Israel:* According to David Tiede says that closure of the mission to Israel as impossible for Luke, on account of his awareness of scriptural promises regarding Israel's salvation. Tiede notes that Luke presents Jesus from the beginning as one set for the fall and rise of many in Israel.[437]
c) *Mission to Gentiles completes mission to Israel:* Jacob Jervell offers third proposal that Luke does not present the mission to Israel as a failure, but as a great success.[438] Joseph Fitzmyer, for instance, follows Jervell in asserting that there is no thought in Acts of promises to Israel being transferred to Gentile Christianity.[439]

Therefore, Gentiles are to be welcomed into the community of salvation on equal terms with Jews. Several significant pieces of evidence could be enlisted in support: Paul's self-description as a "preacher of circumcision" (Gal 5:11), surely a reference to a pre-Damascus interest in making proselytes; his emphasis on the equal status of Jew and Gentile (Rom 10:12),[440] together with his equally firm insistence that Gentile Christians are part

---

436 Blair, "Paul's Call to the Gentile Mission," 19-33.

437 Donaldson, *Paul and the Gentiles*, 250.

438 Jack T. Sanders, *Jews in Luke-Acts* (Philadelphia: Fortress Press, 1987), 317.

439 David L. Tiede, "Glory to Thy People Israel: Luke-Acts and Jews," *in Luke-Acts and Jewish People*, ed. By Tyson 21-34. Cf. Tiede, Prophecy and History in Luke-Acts (Philadelphia: Fortress Press, 1980).

440 Jacob Jervell, "Luke and People of God," in *A New Look at Luke-Acts* (Minneapolis: Augsburg Publishing House, 1972), 1-7.

of Abraham's "seed" (Gal 3: Rom 4).[441] According to Anthony B. Robinson and Robert W. Wall Luke consistently emphasizes the community-its life and its formation.[442]

However, Arland J. Hultgren concludes that we cannot probe the depths of what Paul himself experienced, and we cannot know from Paul himself what, if anything, he experienced in terms of verbal communication concerning his commissioning as an apostle. But it is possible to explore certain non-verbal factors that would have led him to sense the urgency of a mission to the Gentiles.[443]

In addition, from his pre-apostolic past Paul would have known that the Scriptures of Israel anticipate the ingathering of the Gentile nations into the people of God in the messianic age. Such streams of first-hand knowledge and tradition could attend whatever Paul experienced, resulting in his specific vocation as apostle to the Gentiles.[444] Therefore, for Paul, preaching the gospel to the Gentiles was a necessity, indeed it was a commission and thus not of Paul's own will. By doing this work he maintains the freedom to choose the path of his servanthood.[445]

3.10 Law and its Significance at Antioch

Paul and his team took the step of reaching beyond the borders of the Jewish people; they did so with requiring observance of the Jewish Law. However, the reaction of firmly observant Christian Jews sought to require observance of the Law. At the end of the

---

441 Joseph Fitzmyer, "The Jewish People and the Mosaic Law in Luke-Acts," *In Luke the Theologian*, 175-202.

442 Lloyd Gaston, "Paul and the Torah," in *Antisemitism and the Foundations of Christianity,* ed. Alan T. Davies (New York: Pauhst, 1979), 61-62.

443 F. F. Bruce, *Commentary on Galatians* (Grand Rapids: William B. Eerdmans Publishing Company, 1982), 236.

444 Anthony B. Robinson and Robert W. Wall, *Called to Be Church: The Book of Acts for a New Day* (Michigan: William B. Eerdmans Publishing Company, 2006), 79-81.

445 Arland J. Hultgren, "Paul's Christology and His Mission to the Gentiles," in *Paul as Missionary: Identity, Activity, Theology and Practice*, eds. Trevor J. Burke and Brian S. Rosner (London: T & T Claek, 2011), 126-127.

struggle at Antioch, it was victory for the Mission to the Gentiles, for the law free faith characteristic of that mission.[446] Dunn notes the importance of the question of who was and who was not an acceptable table companion. The conclusion still resolves around the food; Dunn even brings specific purity concerns to bear. Thus, the food practices of one group are judged objectionable according to the norms of another group looking on. Dunn suggests that at Antioch, probably for the first time, Paul clearly realized that justification by faith extended beyond acceptance of the Gospel to regulating the life style of the Christ-believers.[447]

Philip Esler says that, "the issue was not precisely that the food was objectionable but hos it was eaten in the mixed social setting of Antioch. Sanders and Dunn say, "for Paul, in fact, the 'the truth of the Gospel' means the freedom with which his Israelites and Gentile converts can be the members of the same congregation without having their 'freedom replaced with the demand of the Mosaic Law."[448] Paul thus concluded that the covenantal nomism of Judaism and of the Jewish believers was in fact a contradiction of that agreed understanding of Justification through faith. To live life "in Christ" and "in accordance with the law" was not possible; it involved a basic contradiction and in the understanding of what made someone acceptable to God. To begin with the Spirit and through faith rules out not just justification by works of Law, but life lived by Law also-the very argument which Paul develops in the rest of Galatians.[449]

---

446 Hultgren, "Paul's Christology and His Mission to the Gentiles,"... 126-127.

447 Kenneth E. Bailey, *Paul through Mediterranean Eyes: Cultural Studies in 1 Corinthians* (Illinois: IVP Academic, 2011), 251-252.

448 Mark D. Nanos, eds., *The Galatians Debate: Contemporary Issues in Rhetorical and Historical Interpretation* (Massachusetts: Hendrickson Publishers, 2002), 348-349.

449 Nanos,*The Galatians Debate*..., 298.

3.11 The New Perspective on Paul

The new perspective on Paul, (here after NPP) is a system of thought in New Testament scholarship that seeks to reinterpret the Apostle Paul and his Letters. It is a direct reaction against what some consider a misunderstanding of Paul by Martin Luther. Luther believed that much of Paul's theology was grounded in an attack against Jews trying to be justified through works, thereby, earning their "right-standing with God"- a conclusion that has been influential in nearly all post-reformation New Testament scholarship.[450] The NPP comes into forefront for debate in the New Testament studies after E.P. Sanders' publication of *Paul and Palestinian Judaism* in 1977.[451]

His main thesis was that the long held view of looking at Paul through "Lutheran-colored spectacles" was incorrect.[452] The NPP is based on the assertion that Second Temple Judaism was a religion of Grace. This assertion is foundation of the NPP.[453] The Phrase "New Perspective on Paul" is coined by Dunn in 4 Nov. 1982 in the Manson Memorial lecture at the University of Manchester.[454] Apart from him E.P. Sanders and N.T. Wright are another popular scholars.

3.11.1 E.P. Sanders

After E.P. Sanders publishes his book Paul and Palestinian Judaism (1997) he receives a wider hearing than his predecessors, and out of which the NPP has been arisen. Sanders examines a wide variety of Jewish sources. He first surveys the early Rabbinic literature from the period between the fall of Jerusalem (AD 70) and the compilation of the Mishnah (AD200). He then looks at portions of

450 Nanos, *The Galatians Debate...*, 299.

451 Nanos, *The Galatians Debate...*, 298.

452 Rich Hagopian, "To be Right with God: An Exploration of the New Perspective View on Paul," *Ashland Theological Journal* (2005): 19.

453 Robert L. Thomas, "Hermeneutics of the New Perspective on Paul,"*The Master Seminary Journal* 16/2 (Fall 2005): 294.

454 Hagopian, "To be Right with God," 19.

the Dead Sea Scrolls and a selection of material from apocryphal and pseudepigraphical writings.[455]

From this lengthy survey, he demonstrates that Judaism has always been first and foremost a religion of grace, with human obedience understood as response to that grace. He also argues that the Judaism of Paul's time was not a religion in which one must seek to gain acceptance with God through acquiring personal merit through good works. Instead, the Jews of Paul's day were taught to keep the law out of gratitude to God for his mercies. The covenant had been given freely by divine initiative, and the law provided the framework for life within the covenant. Doing the law was a means of staying in the covenant. Obedience does not earn acceptance; it simply maintains acceptance. Sanders calls this pattern of religion "covenantal nomism."[456]

3.11.1.1 Covenantal Nomism

It became a key formula for the NPP. It is the view that one's place in God's plan is established on the basis of the covenant and that the covenant requires as the proper response of man his obedience to its commandments, while providing means of atonement from transgression.[457] The pattern or structure of covenantal nomism is this:1) God has chosen Israel and 2) given the law. The law implies both 3) God's promise to maintain the election and 4) the requirement to obey 5) God rewards obedience and punishes transgression. 6) The law provides for means of atonement, and atonement results in 7) maintenance or re-establishment of the covenantal relationship. 8) All those who are maintained in the covenant by obedience, atonement and God's mercy belongs

455 Jeffery Smith, "An Overview and Critique of the New Perspective on Paul's Doctrine of Justification: Part two-the New Perspective Critiqued (1)," *Reformed Baptist Theological Review 111.1* (January, 2006): 118.

456 Nijay K. Gupta, "James D.G. Dunn and the New Perspective on Paul: A Review Article," *Ashland Theological Journal* (2009): 137.

457 Smith, "An Overview and Critique of the New Perspective on Paul's Doctrine of Justification: (Part I)," 82-83.

to the group which will be saved.[458] He adds, "An important interpretation of the first and last points is that election and ultimately salvation are considered to be by God's mercy rather than human achievement.[459]

3.11.1.2 Transfer Terminology

For Sanders the language of justification is "transfer terminology." The transfer is not only from the uncleanness of idolatry and sexual immortality to cleanness and holiness, but from one lordship to another. The transfer takes place by participation in Christ's death.[460] To be justified is to enter into the covenant people. The distinction between "getting in" and "staying in" is important in this regard.

The debate between "faith" and "law," he writes, is a debate about entry requirements, not about life subsequent to conversion. The law is excluded as an entry requirement into the body of those who will be saved; entrance must be by faith apart from the law. Once Gentiles are "in," however, they must behave appropriately and fulfill the law in order to retain their status. Elements of the law which create social distinctions between Jews and Gentiles-circumcision, Sabbath-keeping, food-laws-also has to be discarded, even though Paul never sought a rational explanation for such a selective use of the law.[461]

3.11.1.3 Soteriology

Sanders argues that contrary to the view of protestant Interpreters first century Palestinian Judaism was not and had never been a religion of 'works-righteousness,' by which is meant a religion in which meritorious works automatically earn one's salvation.[462]

458 Smith, "An Overview and Critique of the New Perspective on Paul's Doctrine of Justification: (Part I)," 83-84.

459 E.P. Sanders, *Paul and Palestinian Judaism: A Comparison of Pattern of Religion* (London: SCM Press LTD, 1997), 75.

460 Sanders, *Paul and Palestinian Judaism*, 422.

461 Sanders, *Paul and Palestinian Judaism*, 422.

462 Sanders, *Paul and Palestinian Judaism*, 468.

According to Sanders, salvation comes by membership in the covenant community and by atonement provided for every transgression.[463] Jews emphasized God's free election of Israel rather than earning divine favor by their works of obedience to his law. They were made members of the elected people of God by grace alone. Salvation was a gift, not something they had to first earn.[464]

E. P. Sanders argues that second temple Jews believed, not in a "works-based" salvation but in a "Grace-based" salvation. Now certainly this "grace-based" salvation was not the same as the "salvation by grace through faith" which the reformation teachers spoke of. It was grace-based" in that they understood that collective Israel was chosen, or elected, purely on the basis of God's grace and not on the basis of the people within Israel being special. Being part of the community of Israel, having the scriptures and the covenants (particularly the Mosaic Law), and having the "badges" of that covenant (such as circumcision), led to the idea of identifying Jewish righteousness with these outward things.[465]

Sanders claims that for Paul the only things wrong with Judaism was that it was not Christianity.[466] Claiming that Judaism is not enough he says, "Paul in fact explicitly denies that the Jewish covenant can be effective for salvation, thus consciously denying the basis of Judaism.... More important, the covenantal promises to Abraham do not apply to his descendants, but to Christians."[467] The centre of Paul's thought was not justification, nor his critique

---

463 Mark M. Mattison, A Summary of the New Perspective on Paul, n.p.

464 Daniel Boyarin, *A Radical Jews: Paul and the Politics of Identity* (Los Angeles: University of California Press, 1994), 43.

465 Sanders, *Paul and Palestinian Judaism*, 147. And, Thomas, "Hermeneutics of the New Perspective on Paul," 297.

466 Kent L. Yinger, *The New Perspective on Paul: An Introduction* (Eugene, Oregon: Cascade Book, 2011), 8.

467 Sanders, *Paul and Palestinian Judaism*, 147-148.

of Israel, but was "participation," which focuses on "being in Christ."[468]

Therefore, for Paul, Sanders asserts that Christianity becomes a new form of covenantal nomism, a covenantal religion which one enters by baptism, membership in which provides salvation, which has a specific set of commandments; obedience and repentance keep one in the covenantal relationship, while repeated or heinous transgression removes one from membership.[469] From the above discussion we can perceive that Sanders' stand is Judaism was never a religion of legalism but of God's grace found in the covenant.

3.11.2 James D.G. Dunn

Dunn accepts fully Sanders' interpretation of Palestinian Judaism. He believes that Sanders proves conclusively that first-century Judaism did not teach a doctrine that salvation is earned by the merit of good works. Thus, he agrees with Sanders that the reformation understanding of Paul's doctrine of justification was wrong. Dunn's NPP attempts to interpret Paul's theology in more continuity with his Jewish covenantal roots and correct and complicate the prevailing presumption that Paul was "great exponent of the central reformation doctrine of Justification by faith."[470] For him Gal 2:16 is the most obvious place to start any attempt to take a fresh look at Paul from NPP, as this is probably the first time in Paul's letters that his major theme of Justification by faith sounded.[471]

3.11.2.1 Justification

For Dunn justification by faith is important because of it central significance for formulating the gospel, testing theology and

468 Boyarin, *A Radical Jews: Paul and the Politics of Identity*, 43.

469 Sanders, *Paul and Palestinian Judaism*, 552.

470 N.T. Wright, *What Saint Paul Really Said: Was Paul of Tarsus the Real Founder of Christianity?* (Grand Rapids: William B. Eerdmans Publishing Company, 1997), 19.

471 Sanders, *Paul and Palestinian Judaism*, 513.

reappraising Christianity's Jewish roots and heritage. The doctrine of justification by faith, which has proved so luminous over four centuries of protestant theology in particular, has the capacity to provide fresh illumination in the present (and no doubt future) reassessment of Paul's theology.[472] He argues that the reformation was wrong on its claim that Paul's teaching on justification was a reaction against and in opposition to Judaism. As Luther had rejected a medieval church which offered salvation by merit and good works, the same, it was assumed, was true of Paul in relation to Judaism of his day.[473]

Basing on Gal 2:16, Dunn claims that justification is a Jewish covenantal category referring to "God's recognition of Israel as his people, his verdict in favor of Israel on grounds of his covenant with Israel."[474]

The problem that Paul addresses is not the problem of legalism and not earning acceptance of God by good works, but rather Jewish exclusivism expressed in the insistence that Gentile Christians adhere to certain boundary marking regulations such as circumcision, Sabbath and food laws. Justification is about erasing ethnic boundaries between Jews and Gentiles by declaring that all who believe in Christ and are faithful to him are in the covenant.[475] Here the distinctiveness of Paul's Gospel also can be seen in his theology of Justification of faith.[476]

3.11.2.2 Work of the Law

Lutheran scholarship has traditionally set gospel and law in sharp antithesis and attributed the antithesis wholly to Paul. But Dunn says that Paul reasserts the importance of keeping the laws of God. He assumed up all the commandments into the love commandment

---

472 James D.G.Dunn, *The New Perspective on Paul the Apostle* (Grand Rapids: William B. Eerdmans Publishing Company, 2005), 101.

473 Dunn, *The New Perspective on Paul the Apostle*, 105.

474 James D.G. Dunn, *Theology of Paul the Apostle* (Grand Rapids: William B. Eerdmans Publishing Company, 1998), 340.

475 Dunn, *Theology of Paul*, 335-336.

476 Yinger, *The New Perspective on Paul: An Introduction*, 20.

(Ram 13:9; Gal 5:14).[477] Therefore, building on Sanders' work, Dunn's major contribution to NPP is laid on his understanding of "work of the law."[478] Dunn argues that this phrase refers not to works-righteousness but to particular observances of the law that functioned as badges of Jewish identity in the ancient world.[479] Dunn strengthens his idea by finding similar usage of the phrase in other Jewish writings. Thus, a number of the Dead Sea Scrolls used the Hebrews equivalent to "work of Law," to describe the sect's distinctive practices. By these practices, these "work of law," it became clear who did, and who did not, belong to the sect.[480]

Michael Thompson, summarizes Dunn's work on 'work of law' saying,

> Dunn's major contribution consists in his view that the "work of the law" Paul opposed in Galatians primarily referred to circumcision... keeping the religious calendar... and observing the dietary laws... that distinguished Jews from Gentiles. Drawing on insights from sociology, Dunn calls these particular "work of the law" the badges or boundary markers of Judaism. Paul opposed these practices because they functioned to separate people whom Christ died to bring together... in short, Paul's target was not an insistence on basic moral behavior, but on particular religious practices that differentiated Jews from Gentiles, demonstrating the former group's status a members within God's covenant.[481]

---

477 Smith, "An Overview and Critique of the New Perspective on Paul's Doctrine of Justification: (Part I)," 87.

478 James D.G. Dunn, *Jesus, Paul and the Gospels Apostles* (Grand Rapids: William B. Eerdmans Publishing Company, 2011), 103.

479 Dunn, *Jesus, Paul and the Gospels Apostles*, 113-114.

480 Smith, "An Overview and Critique of the New Perspective on Paul's Doctrine of Justification: (Part I)," 86-87.

481 Yinger, *The New Perspective on Paul: An Introduction*, 20.

Where Paul differed fundamentally from his Jewish tradition was not over the role of Grace, faith and obedience in salvation, but whether salvation was tied to being Jewish or not.[482] As Paul used the phrase "not by work of the law" to differentiate his position from his opponents, it is clear for Dunn that 'work of law' could simply be the way in which one group is identified; and the justification or salvation no longer comes by identification with the Torah-party, but with Christ in faith.

3.11.3 Nicholas Thomas Wright (N. T. Wright)

N.T. Wright has been a major force in the spread of NPP. In fact, he has used the phrase eve before Dunn in a 1978 article, in which he offered "a new way of looking at Paul which provides... a new perspective on other related Pauline problems." Wright's work constitutes a chief expression of the NPP. One of the characteristics of his position is how he sets Paul's theology within the larger biblical story (narrative) of God's work with Israel.[483] Wright's focus is the gospel and the doctrine of justification.

3.11.3.1 The Gospel

He demonstrates that the core of Paul's gospel was not justification by faith, but the death and resurrection of Christ and his exaltation as Lord. The proclamation of the Gospel was the proclamation of Jesus as Lord, the Messiah who fulfilled Israel's expectations.[484]

He says, "When Paul refers to 'the gospel,' he is referring to the demonstrated to be both Israel's Messiah and the World's true Lord."[485] The gospel is the announcement that Jesus is Lord- Lord of the Lord, Lord of the cosmos, Lord of the earth, of the ozone layer, of whales and waterfall, of trees and tortoises.[486]

482 Yinger, *The New Perspective on Paul: An Introduction*, 21.

483 Smith, "An Overview and Critique of the New Perspective (Part I)," 86.

484 Yinger, *The New Perspective on Paul: An Introduction*, 21.

485 Yinger, *The New Perspective on Paul: An Introduction*, 27.

486 Mattison, "A Summary of the New Perspective on Paul."

3.11.3.2 Doctrine of Justification

Some of the characteristics of his teaching as it relates to the doctrine of justification can be summarized as follows: first, Wright agrees with Sanders' basic interpretation of 2nd temple Judaism. He writes," serious modification may be required but we regard his basic pint as established."[487] Describing this "basic point" he says, "Judaism in Paul's day was not… a religion of legalistic works-righteousness."[488]

Second, Wright generally agrees with Dunn regarding "the works of the Law." He defines this expression as "the badges of Jewish race."[489] He claims that for Paul, "covenant membership is defined, not by the works of the law but by faith in Christ."[490]

Third, he insists that justification is a covenant term that means to be recognized as a covenant member. In this case, to be "righteous" means to be faithful to the covenant or to be a covenant member. And to be "justified" is to be declared by God as a member of his true covenant family. Wright repeatedly says that the doctrine of justification in improperly placed in the realm of soteriology. Its proper place is in the realm of ecclesiology.[491]

Fourth, Wright, like other NPP, argues that "the righteousness of God" should be understood as "God's covenant with faithful people" rather than God's on righteousness and status of righteousness which human have before.[492] Righteousness from the human side simply means covenant membership, while the righteousness of God refers to His covenant faithfulness to His promises and to His people.[493]

Fifth, faith is effectively the basis of justification. Thus, on the basis of the faith produced in the heart by the spirit we are

---

487 Wright, *What Saint Paul Really Said*, 152.

488 Wright, *What Saint Paul Really Said*, 153-154.

489 Wright, *What Saint Paul Really Said*, 20.

490 Wright, *What Saint Paul Really Said*, 18-19.

491 Wright, *What Saint Paul Really Said*, 120.

492 Wright, *What Saint Paul Really Said*, 129.

493 Wright, *What Saint Paul Really Said*, 105-106.

recognized as covenant members, or we are justified. One might even say that we are justified by faith alone, but certainly not in the sense that reformers meant this. Faith is not merely the receptive instrument by which chrit and His righteousness are received. It is the badge by which we are recognized to be members of God's people.[494]

Sixth, Wright sometimes speaks of faith as amounting to the same thing as faithfulness. He says "One of Paul's key phrases is 'the obedience of faith'. Faith and obedience are not antithetical. They belong exactly together. Indeed, very often the word faith itself could properly be translated as faithfulness."[495]

Seventh, denying the reformed doctrine of the imputation of the righteousness of Christ to the believer, Wright says that justification functions like the verdict in the law court: by acquitting someone, it confers on the person the status righteous.[496] For him, "Righteousness is not an object, a substance or a gas which can be passed across the courtroom... To imagine the defendant somehow receiving the judge's righteousness is simply a category mistake."[497]

Eight, in relation to eschatology he argues that the covenant declaration is ultimately to be made at the end of history. The events of the last day were anticipated when Jesus died on the cross and rose again. The verdict of the last day is therefore now also anticipated in the present, whether somehow believes in Gospel message about Jesus.[498]

3.12 Some Critiques of NPP

Robert L. Thomas argues that the sources cited by Sanders reveals Sanders' reading of the rabbinic material is totally biased. For instance, Sanders took only one reason that election was totally gratuitous for Israel's earning election. He neglected other two

494 Wright, *What Saint Paul Really Said*, 100.

495 Smith, "An Overview and Critique of the New Perspective (Part I)," 89.

496 Smith, "An Overview and Critique of the New Perspective (Part I)," 91.

497 Wright, *What Saint Paul Really Said*, 160.

498 Wright, *What Saint Paul Really Said*, 131.

reasons where election grounded on the merits of the patriarchs and Israel's foreseen obedience.[499] It is claimed that there is a lot of Jewish literature that Sanders never dealt with which gives a much more legalistic picture of Judaism. This leads Sanders to argue that Judaism was a religion of grace. It is soundly contradicted by the NT itself. Surely in attempting to understand the Judaism of that day, the NT should be included as one of our major sources.[500]

While Sanders used rabbinic materials he did not make such use of the historical accounts of the New Testament like four gospels and Acts, and some of the Pauline writings have also been set aside, ignoring important passages like Eph 2:8-9; 2 Tim 3:5-7, which support the traditional viewpoint.[501]

Robert L. Thomas again says that NPP repeatedly violate the hermeneutical principle of giving closest attention to the immediate context of a given passage. They invariably jump from passage to passage without a thorough consideration of the various contexts. That result in violation of the original author's intention and the original reader understands of what was written.[502]

New perspective proponents seem to have lost sight of the fact that the Judaism of Jesus' day was not the religion of the OT. It was largely a product of Israel's captivity years in Babylon.[503]

Jeffery Smith, raised the question on its implication if the NPP is right, then the reformation was wrong. Thus, our confession of faith is wrong. The whole protestant reformation was a big mistake. This also shakes the understanding of the Bible and the Gospels.[504]

---

499 Wright, *What Saint Paul Really Said*, 98.

500 Wright, *What Saint Paul Really Said*, 131.

501 Thomas, "Hermeneutics of the New Perspective on Paul," 296.

502 Smith, "An Overview and Critique of the New Perspective (Part II)," 125-126.

503 Thomas, "Hermeneutics of the New Perspective on Paul," 298.

504 Thomas, "Hermeneutics of the New Perspective on Paul," 308.

Summary

Defining Christian identity is not an easy task without understanding Paul's Christological and missiological framework. How Paul does describe the divinity and humanity of Jesus Christ sets a stage on which we can develop the Christian identity. It noticed that there is an absence of any references to Jesus as son of man in Paul's Christology. In this sense Paul is distinct from the gospels. But it can be argued that the most distinct aspect of Paul's Christology is his last Adam typology. Paul's last Adam Christology draws on Genesis, while the son of man material in the gospels draws on Daniel 7. In short, the last Adam Christology is more universal than the son of man in scope. By comparing and contrasting Christ with the progenitor of the whole human race Paul forged a concept in which both Jews and Gentiles/Nations had a stake simple because they were human.

Paul's concept of eschatology was an ongoing process of New Testament theology. His eschatology is centered on Christ who would come to judge the living and the death. Some Scholars have found two un-reconciled types of eschatology; one is a collective which is rooted in Jewish apocalyptic and represented in I & II Thessalonians and I Corinthians, and the other one is an individual approach emphasizing personal development and set forth in Philippians and Colossians. Some interpreters have seen in the language of this final reconciliation a "universal homecoming" interpreted in terms of a universal salvation of all sentient creatures, both human and angelic.[505]

Albert Schweitzer view eschatology as a final event, where the whole cosmos will be affected by this event. And he critics that Paul's teaching by saying that the dying and rising of the believers puts one in a position of advantage over the other. He also differs from Paul's theology of pneumatology for he asserts that the spirit that resurrected Christ was already at work within the created world and in this thereby the Spirit as an advocate send

505 Thomas, "Hermeneutics of the New Perspective on Paul," 301-304.

at the ascension of Christ is blurred and ignored and therefore Jesus Christ become a mere human who was the first of a kind to resurrect.

To sum up, Albert Schweitzer finds the solution to all his Biblical problems by the thorough, consistent application of eschatology as the fundamental framework which alone makes possible a unified comprehension of Christian thought up until Greek theology. For this reason his thought has been termed 'Consistent Theology.'

The two hymns provide that the faith community should continue in faith stable and steadfast, not shifting from the hope of the gospel which is heard, which has been preached to every creature because Christ is first born of creation, wisdom and the last Adam who brought salvific good news to everyone. Paul also clearly makes some very exalted claims about Jesus. He is the Lord, exalted to a unique position of power and authority to God's right hand; he is the embodiment of the divine Wisdom itself, and Jesus perhaps can be spoken of as pre-existent; he is invoked and venerated by other human beings.

The NPP attempts to understand Paul and theology against the background of the so called Second Temple Judaism or first century Judaism and also stresses similarities and continuities between Judaism and Christianity. Though it can be assumed that all the scholars of NPP may not agree on everything regarding Paul and Judaism, Wright and Dunn have laid down the main lines of what has become known as the NPP, sometimes simply referred to as the (Sanders) Dunn-wright-trajectory.

The main lines of NPP should be: 1. First century Judaism was not legalistic, but was characterized by covenantal nomism-saved by God's grace and obligated to follow his ways. 2. Since Jews were not espousing works-righteousness, Paul was not opposing legalism in his letters. 3. Paul does not differ from most other Jews as to the roles of grace, faith and works in salvation; where he differs is the conviction that Jesus is Israel's Messiah and the Lord of all creation. No longer is Torah the defending center of God's dealing; what counts now is belonging to Christ.

We can also discern that the NPP brings the right perspective for the New Testament study especially on Paul arguing reformation theologians on their understanding of Paul's theology as against Jews trying to earn salvation through work. But on the other hand we can say that NPP is supportive of the central slogans of the reformation like justification by faith alone, by scripture alone and salvation through Christ alone and not by work. The New Perspective and understanding on the theology of Paul, especially on the particular topic of grace, salvation, justification and work of law given by the NPP makes a new history in the history of the New Testament studies.

Chapter 4

Reinterpreting Paul's Confrontation with Peter in the Light of Redefinition of Christian Identity in a Pluralistic Context

Introduction

Redefining Christian identity is a conglomerated task in a religiously pluralistic society like India. In such a society, Christianity was been accepted by numbers of people irrespective of their social indifferences. But still converts experience identical crisis inside the fold of Christianity. Is it due to the caste system or due to the lack of role models? Can Antioch's incident be interpreted in the light of pluralistic context? What types of new identity can be formulate? Can Antioch's incident be a paradigm for Indian context where people have various social and religious indifferences? How do eating habits signify various cultures? Moreover, how does the Christian identity survive under the threat of Hindutva? How does the fundamentalist treat Christianity? These are the few questions that have been discussed in this chapter.

4.1 Religious Pluralism in India

India is well known for its religious plurality and cultural diversity. In such a web of religious plurality conversion and its related issues are most sensitive because it causes cultural and religious dislocation and re-socialization. On the one hand religious pluralism provides both opportunity and challenge with regard to Christian identity and conversion and help us to cross over the identical boundaries. In this context religious identity means not only a stand or shift from one religion to another, but also a shift from one community to another or crossing of religious boundaries. 'Conversion to Christianity in India means not only change of a religion but also stepping into an utterly strange religious and social milieu.'[506]

This new socio-religious location creates confusion in the minds of converts and they face the most significant change in their lives. It means leaving behind their own cultural heritage and accepting a new identity where style of worship and faith components is different. Moreover, issue of religious identity becomes more complex due to confusion over role model; who is the role model for new converts? Text like Galatians 2:11-21 creates dilemma in the minds of converts and many ties it becomes hurdles for them to make right choice. Hindus see conversion in sociological and political terms whereas Christians see it in theological terms.[507]

4.2 Caste System and Its Impact on Society

Dawn to the centuries it has been observed and witnessed that caste system has created social imbalance and changed the status quo which led many outcaste and Tribal voluntarily accept other religion particularly Christianity. However, the status of converts did not change even after accepting new religion due to the existence of caste system in Christianity as well. Dalit and Tribal

---

506 Smith, "An Overview and Critique of the New Perspective (Part I)," 107-108.

507 G. E. Ladd, *A Theology of the New Testament,* 568.

had accepted Christianity in order to get rid of the hegemonic caste system and *karmasamsara*[508] but the identity remained same. Converts are known by Dalit Christian or Tribal Christians. Massive conversion took place among Dalits communities like Paraiyars, Pulaiyars, Chakkiraiyars, Pallans, Mahars, Malas and Madiga in south. In North Bhangis and Chamars of Uttar Pradesh, Chuhras of Punjab, and Mahars of Maharashtra came to Christianity.[509]

Seeing such influx of Dalit to Christianity through mass movement, Gandhi too believed that "it is conversion for convenience"[510] and not genuine conversion. Therefore, converts are still struggling for their Identity in Christianity. What could be their Identity? Why have they not been treated equally in church? It is reminds us the Antioch where arguments had happened due the identity: Jews or Gentiles. In a similar way converts in India are facing identical crisis. Church is not free from the caste system. Paul and Peter were both the representative of different groups and their arguments was all about the Identity for the new converts.

4.3 Hindu Nationalism and Its Ideology

The issue if Christian identity has been exacerbated by the rapid growth of various Hindu nationalist movements, their campaign to uphold Hindutva and their idcology of rejecting anything foreign on Indian soil. The inspiration behind this Hindutava ideology can be traced back to Swami Dayanand Saraswati, who urged a regeneration of Hindus through adherence to a purified Vedic faith. He established *Arya Samaj* with the aim of reviving Hindu doctrines. His motto was "back to Vedas" and *Aryavarta* for the Aryans.[511] It is precisely this view that equated Indian culture with

508 Kim, *In Search of Identity*, 4-5.

509 Kim, *In Search of Identity*, 4-5.

510 It refers to the cycle of birth and rebirth as a result of one's action.

511 Robert Eric Frykenberg, "Gospel, Globalization and Hindutva: The Policies of Conversion in India," in *Christianity Reborn: The Global Expansion of Evangelism in the Twentieth Century*, edited by Donald M. Lewis (Grand Rapids: William B. Eerdmans Publishing Company, 2004), 122.

Hinduism and Hindu culture and constitutes the core of the Sang Parivaar.

As a result of this strong cultural nationalism, Hindu fundamentalist groups are now actively seeking to reconvert Indian Christians back to Hinduism and to restore them to religious purity through the rite of *Gharvapsi* or *Shuddhi*, which they interpret as 'homecoming' and Sanskritization.[512] Not only this, even history is now being rewritten to suit Hindu nationalism. The educational system is hijacked and being redefined in order to influence young minds to believe in Hindutva ideology. Christian identity is seen with suspicion and all social and humanitarian works of Christians are seen as aiming towards conversion, to destabilize the socio-cultural fabric and security of India and to reduce the Hindus to minority.

Furthermore, since 1980s and 1990s nationalist Hindus began to call for total allegiance from the religious minorities to a common Hindu Identity which necessitated giving up not only their self-identity as a community but also their individual faith as Christians.[513] All these prove that Hindu nationalists are trying to redefine India solely in terms of monocultural Hindu *Rastra* (Nation). Amidst such a scenario which is complex, where does Christian identity stand and how could it be possible to redefine it.

4.4 Eating Habits in India and Socio-Cultural Dynamism

We cannot live without eating. Even more remarkable, eating is a spiritual practice. We are reminded by the testimonies of various scriptures and their spiritual heritage that eating and drinking are not merely responses to physical hunger but in them something

512 Cited in George Oommen, "Conversion in India: A Historical Appraisal with Reference to M.K. Gandhi's Response to Conversion," *BTF* 32/1 (June, 2000): 159.

513 S.M. Michael, "Culture, Nation, Conversion: Issues for Mission," in *The Church in India in the Emerging Third Millennium*, edited by Fr. Thomas D'Sa (Bangalore: NBCLC, 2005), 230.

else also happens that satisfies the deepest longings of our souls.[514] Moreover, eating habits define our socio-cultural and religious identity. Various religious traditions in India in which eating habits are different communicate that meal matters and matters deeply and in all them it symbolizes various type of meanings. Due to the limitation of this research, North Indian context has been given preference to locate the significance of eating habits and what type of socio-cultural dynamism can be located.

4.4.1 *Sangat*[515] in Sikhism: The Common Gathering for eating and fellowship

The common gathering for devotion, *sangat* is eventually associated with *langar that* is a key feature in all the Gurdwaras where people eat together irrespective of their caste, creed, class, gender, religion and nationality.[516] It was instituted to break the system of caste and to bring unity and equality among people. "The culture of *langar* expresses the ethics of sharing, community, inclusiveness and oneness of all humankind."[517]

Langar cannot be separated from *sangat*. In *langar* everyone is expected to participate and it is *langar* that leads to participate in common devotion because God is one and there is no high and low or rich and poor in the sight of God. As in *langar* so in *sangat* all people are invited to pray and praise God irrespective of any discrimination. It shows the unity of humankind as well as the hospitable nature of God who never discriminates. The idea behind to introduce the *sangat* system was that in the company of righteous the unrighteous will be changed because in *sangat*

514 "Sanskritization" is a term coined by M.N. Srinivas to refer to the process by which lower castes attain higher positions in the caste system by adopting Sanskkritic values. See M.N. Srinivas, *Caste in Modern India and Other Essays* (New Delhi: Asia Publishing House, 1962), 42.

515 Kim, *In Search of Identity*, 192.

516 Gordon T. Smith, *A Holy Meal: The Lord's Supper in the Life of the Church* (Michigan: Baker Academics, 2005), 9.

517 The community meeting place for the Sikh people.

only the seeker of truth will join.[518] Thus, the hospitable aspect comes out in Trinitarian understanding: one community in unity and equality, liberating and guiding spirit for moral and spiritual inspiration.[519] *Pangat* and *Sangat* both the customs were brought up to eliminate the immoral practice of untouchability in the society and have become most hospitable practices in Indian society.

4.4.2 Eating Habits in Hinduism

Although Hinduism has few dietary laws, eating habits are influenced by religious belief, by caste regulations, and particularly by concepts of purity and pollution.[520] A major area of influence on eating habits is that of caste. Traditionally, a Hindu should not accept food, especially cooked food, from some one of a lower caste, since the food would be polluted: any food which another person touches or smells is really polluted, but cooked food is particularly vulnerable to the essence of the person cooking it. The danger of pollution is far greater from cooked than uncooked food. Though the custom is now dying out, it used to be common sense to employ only Brahmin cooks and waiters in a restaurant, because anyone can eat the food prepared by a Brahmin.[521]

Hinduism does not explicitly prohibit eating meat, but it does strongly recommend *Ahimsa* – the concept of non-violence against all life forms including animals. As a consequence, many Hindus prefer vegetarian or lacto-vegetarian lifestyle and methods of food production that is in harmony with nature and compassionate, respectful of other life forms as well as nature.[522]

---

518 Chris Shannahan, *A Theology of Community Organizing: Power to the People* (New York: Routledge, 2014), 147.

519 Sardar Harjeet Singh, *Faith and Philosophy of Sikhism...*, 230.

520 Dalbir Singh Dhillon, *Sikhism: Origin and Development,* New Delhi: Atlantic Publishers & Distributers, 1988, 199.

521 Nikky-Guninder Kaur Singh, *Sikhism: An Introduction,* New York: I. B. Tauris, 2011, 88.

522 Jeaneane D. Fowler, *Hinduism: Beliefs and Practices* (Oregon: Sussex Academic Press, 1997), 65.

If the Hindu high case system has been rigid throughout history, the dietary habits of each caste have been equally immutable. You are what you eat is a simple dictum except in India, where it means much more. What you eat dictates who you marry, where you live, your job, your social status, whether you are "dirty" or "clean", whether you are entitled or deprived, and whether you can hold your head high or let it hang in shame, because the food you eat is a function of your caste.[523]

4.5 Christian Identity in India

4.5.1 Religious Persecution and Conversion

In the recent past attacks on minorities particularly Christians and Muslims communities have been increased. *Dadri Kand* in Uttar Pradesh and persecution in North India where Christians are being persecuted and executed, nuns have been raped, Bibles were burnt, churches were demolished and educational institutes are being targeted are some of the recent example of religious persecution. However, under all these pressures the body of Christ still is growing. Sebastian Kim gives four explanations related to the complexity of the issues of conversion in India:[524] (1) problem of communalism, (2) due to conversion challenging the socio-economic establishment like hierarchical caste system, (3) aggressive campaign of Hindu fundamentalists and (4) different understanding of the conversion by Hindus and Christians. Therefore, the issue of conversion in India is related to social, religious, cultural, political and economic aspects.

Conversion in India is all the more sensitive because it tends to disturb the status quo and creates social imbalance.[525] According to V.J. Rajshekhar, upper castes are restoring to Hinduisation of untouchables and Tribals so that Hinduism may continue as the majority religion. He further states that if Untouchables and Tribals who are 30% of Indian population, and 35% backward classes

523 Fowler, *Hinduism...*, 66.

524 Patrick Olivelle, *Manu's Code of Law* (Oxford: Oxford University Press, 2005), 279-280.

525 Olivelle, *Manu's Code of Law*, 280.

who are neither *Shudras* nor Hindus walk out, Hindus will be not only as minority as but less than the population of Muslim which is 15%.[526] This is why conversion is strongly opposed by Hindus. Moreover, it is a means to destroy and uproot the Brahminism.

4.6 Paul's Corporate Christological and Soteriological Framework and Model of Pauline Christianity among Converts in North India

4.6.1 Paul's Corporate Christology

Paul very frequent uses the phrase "in Christ" in his writings.[527] Albert Schweitzer famously saw this "being-in-Christ" as the key to Paul's theology, understanding it as a form of mysticism-Christ mysticism-in which the elect are united in one corporeity with Christ, having died and raised with him.[528] Schweitzer's basic emphasis, though differently nuanced and expressed, remains important to more recent attempts to capture the heart of Pauline thought, such as E.P. Sanders' "participationist eschatology" or Morna Hooker's "interchange."[529] Nevertheless, James Dunn considers that the theme of participation "in Christ" has been somewhat neglected in recent studies of Paul, compared with "the amazingly vigorous contemporary debate on justification by faith."[530]

It has proved difficult to express exactly what kind of "reality" Paul has in mind with the idea of Christians being "in Christ", together comprising the "body of Christ" (1Cor 12:27). Adolf Deissmann famously found it nonsensical to speak of being "in" another person, and concluded that "Paul must have

526 Kim, *In Search of Identity*, 4-5.

527 P. Roy, "Conversion," in *Global Dictionary of Theology*, edited by William A. Dyrness and Veli Matti Karkkainen (Nottingham: IVP, 2008), 200.

528 V.J. Rajshekhar, *Weapons to Fight Counter Revolution* (Bangalore: Dalit Sahtiya Akademy, 2004), 53.

529 G.A. Deissmann, *Paul: A Study in Social and Religious History*, 2nd ed. (London: Hodder & Stoughton, 1926), 140.

530 A. Schweitzer, *the Mysticism of Paul the Apostle*, 2nd ed. (London: A. & C. Black, 1953), 10-19.

thought of Christ as a kind of an impersonal continuum, like the atmosphere."[531] Subsequently interpreters have rejected Deissmann's implausible suggestion, but have remained sympathetic to his perplexity concerning the meaning of the idiom.[532] But in terms of Paul's Christology this much at least is indisputable: Paul describes Jesus not solely in terms of what he as an individual is or has become-Messiah, Lord, Son of God, etc.-but as someone in and through whom believers live, both individually and corporately.[533]

More fruitful perhaps than a focus on what ontological status Paul implies with his "in Christ" language is an attempt to see what this corporate Christology-language does in terms of the construction of Christian identity, and here insights from the social sciences may be of considerable help. The sociology of knowledge approach known most widely through the work of Peter Berger and Thomas Luckmann explores the ways in which everything that passes for "knowledge"-expressed in language, symbols, ideas, etc.-forms a "symbolic universe", a body of tradition which shapes and orders human behavior and relationships.[534] From this perspective, the separation all too evident in Pauline studies, between "doctrinal" subjects such as Paul's Christology or soteriology on the one hand, and his ethics and exhortations on the other, breaks down.

Paul's statements about God, Christ, Spirit and so on, all serve to structure the identity and inter-action of the Christian community. Recent studies informed by this perspective have examined the ways in which even such thoroughly theological symbols as Jesus' death on the cross serve to construct and shape the social praxis of the early Christian communities. In one such study, for example, Raymond Pickett, describing his project as an exercise in "sociological exegesis" and using Berger and

531 E.P. Sanders, *Paul and Palestinian Judaism* (London: SCM, 1977), 549.

532 J.D.G. Dunn, *The Theology of Paul the Apostle* (Edinburgh: T&T Clark, 1998), 395.

533 C.F.D. Moule, *The Origin of Christology* (Cambridge: CUP, 1977), 60.

534 Moule, *The Origin of Christology*, 47-52.

Luckmann's work as a theoretical resource, emphasizes that his concern is to move beyond social and historical description to an analysis of the "social impact" that "a text, or symbol within the text, was designed to have in the realm of social interaction."[535]

Also important is the recent focus on the theme of identity, most developed from a social-scientific point of view in Philip Esler's use of social identity theory in a study of Galatians. Esler uses the work of social psychologist Henri Tajfel to shed light on the ways in which Paul seeks to construct and maintain "the distinctive identity of his congregations in relation to the Israelite and Gentile out-groups."[536]

In a situation of inter-group conflict, Paul is concerned to sustain the boundaries between the Christian community and both Israel on the one hand and the Gentiles on the other, and does so by creating a positive social identity for his converts. One of the benefits of Esler's focus on identity is that it links together both "theological" and "ethical" sections of Paul's letter(s) and highlights their "group-oriented" character: both serve "to maintain and enhance group identity."[537]

We may then valuably focus on Paul's corporate Christology, not out of a concern with his doctrine of Christ per se, nor with the category of "reality" which he has in mind in speaking of believers being in Christ, but rather with a focus on the ways in which this Christology serves to construct Christian identity and community, to shape and pattern relationships. This will hopefully enable us to consider afresh the question as to how, if at all, the identity and conduct of Jew and Gentile are redefined as a consequence of their being "in Christ". In both Galatians and Colossians the declaration is that now "there is no longer Jew and Greek (Gal 3:28; Col 3:11)."[538]

---

535 Moule, *The Origin of Christology*, 52-56.

536 P.L. Berger and T. Luckmann, *The Social Construction of Reality* (London: Penguin, 1967), 113.

537 R. Pickett, *The Cross in Corinth: The Social Significance of the Death of Jesus* (Sheffield: SAP, 1997), 34-35.

538 P.P. Esler, *Galatians* (London and New York: Routledge, 1998), 42.

Commenting on the meaning of the major Christian ritual, the Lord's Supper, Paul similarly stresses that this is a celebration of the unity and oneness of the body of believers who share in the blood and body of Christ: "because there is one bread, we many are one body, for we all partake of the one bread" (1 Cor 10:17). The fact that Paul presents this assertion concisely as an apparently uncontroversial basis for his argument that the Corinthians should avoid with demons (1 Cor 10:20-21) may indicate, as Paul Gardner suggests, that this understanding of the Lord's Supper was widely shared, at least between Paul and the Corinthians.[539] Paul's conviction that the Lord's Supper should demonstrate the oneness of the body of Christians also explains why he is so disturbed by the divisions that currently appear when the Corinthians gather for this meal (1 Cor 11:17-34), and why he considers that such a divided celebration is no longer really the Lord's Supper at all (1 Cor 11:20).[540]

This oneness in Christ, which baptism initiates and the Lord's Supper celebrate, is most vividly and profoundly expressed in Paul's notion of the community as the body of Christ. The functioning human body perfectly illustrates the idea that a group of "members" can be diverse and different, with different functions to perform, yet also be essentially one (1Cor 12:12 27). Paul, of course, goes beyond simply using the human body as an illustration of how a community of diverse people can be united, and actually describes the Christian congregation as "the body of Christ" (1Cor 12:12, 27; cf. Rom 12:5).[541]

From a social-scientific perspective, then, we would expect Paul's corporate Christology-the declaration that all converts are one body in Christ-both to function as a fundamental designation of distinctive group-identity and to structure social interaction

---

539 Esler, *Galatians, 45.*

540 R. Scroggs, *"Paul and the Eschatological Woman,"* JAAR 40 (1972), 283-303.

541 P.D. Gardner, *The Gifts of God and the Authentication of a Christian: An Exegetical Study of 1 Corinthians 8-11:1* (Lanham, New York, London: University Press of America, 1994), 161-165.

within the congregations. However, that leaves open the question as to how, and in what ways, this denning identity affects other aspects of the believers' identity (social, cultural, religious, etc.) and social conduct. The answer to that question cannot be deduced from social-scientific theory but must be drawn from the evidence of Paul's letters. In what ways, we may ask, does this corporate Christology, and the fundamental "Christian" identity which it encapsulates, undergird a redefinition and restructuring of existing identities and practices? To what extent does Paul see his own and others' identities fundamentally redefined by their being in Christ, and is there any evidence that Paul's corporate Christology was controversial-perhaps precisely because of its implications for the social interaction and identity of the Christian congregations?

There is some evidence, then, to support the hypothesis that Paul's corporate Christology was not only distinctive but also to some degree controversial. It appears to represent one point of contrast between Paul (together with the Antioch community, at least prior to the "incident" there) and the varied forms of Jewish Christianity associated with James and the Jerusalem church. Specifically, Paul's corporate Christology seems likely to have underpinned his controversial conviction that, because Jews and Gentiles are together one body in Christ, a new creation, they can and must share unbounded fellowship at the Lord's Table.

Coming to the context of north Indians' converts, the truth of the gospel has been denied throughout the history. Caste and class are some of the most significant key factors of it. In Galatians Paul defense what he call "the truth of the gospel."[542] However, there is no such defense that we can trace out in North Indian context. The Hindu converts do not feel free and comfortable in the fold of Christianity. Hindu converts face discrimination in various forms: one of them is the different eating habits among Hindu converts and Christians. According to Paul, "freedom in Christ" is a gift of God and it is hopeless and fruitless to expect the preservation of

542 D.G. Horrell, *"The Lord's Supper at Corinth and in the Church Today,"* Theology 98 (1995), 196-202.

freedom by those who are not free themselves.[543] The way of the opponents does not secure their salvation in Christ, but destroys it by replacing it with the Jewish concept of salvation.[544]

Paul though it of vital importance to maintain the view that through the gospel Gentiles also were given to participate in the promise to Abraham and inheritance of Abraham.[545] Contrary to this, those who belong to high castes are not interested in quitting their previous traditions because though they are poor but not the oppressed one. That is why 75% of the Christian are from lower or untouchable communities.[546] Interestingly, high caste converts have the privilege to remain as high caste but converts from other communities who embraced Christianity to get out of the suffocating gas chamber of Hinduism, are once again discriminated within the church.[547]

North Indian Christians are the victims of untouchability, casteism, discrimination within the church. For this there are several reasons such as; their state of dependency, their lack of self-respect and their lack of leadership in the church.[548] Therefore from above explanation we can draw a line that Pauline model of Christianity represents corporate aspect, unity among Converts and Christians, no discrimination based on birth, eating habits, rituals and traditions. Pauline model of Christianity also support those who are in Christ Jesus they are new community; a community that represent the body of Christ. Thus, for Paul, Jews and Greeks had become one in Christ (Gal 3:28) and both are "the members of the household faith (Eph 2:19)."[549]

---

543 R.P. Martin, *2 Corinthians* (WBC 40; Waco, TX: Word Books, 1986), 399.

544 Hans Dieter Betz, *Galatians: A Commentary on Paul's Letter to the Churches in Galatia* (Philadelphia: Fortress Press, 1979), 30.

545 Betz, *Galatians...*, 32.

546 Betz, *Galatians...*, 33.

547 James D.G. Dunn, *The Theology of Paul's Letter to the Galatians* (Cambridge: Cambridge University Press, 1994), 40.

548 M. Azariah, *The Un-Christian Side of the Indian Church* (Bangalore: Dalit Sahitya Akademy, 1985), ii.

549 Azariah, *The Un-Christian Side of the Indian Church*, ii.

4.6.2 Paul's Corporate Soteriology

Soteriology is one of the important central theological themes in the theology of Pauline writings for salvation is the very purpose of the incarnation of Son of god (1 Tim 1:15). Salvation is a general notion that helps to pin point his message[550] as we found the idea of salvation throughout his writings.

4.6.2.1 The Meaning of the Term

The term soteriology means doctrine of salvation or, more concretely, the way of salvation, and derives from the Greek σωτηρία.[551] The word σωτηρία means deliverance, perseverance, safety and salvation. It is used to mean deliverance from the milestone of enemies (Acts 7:25); in ethical sense, which conduces to the soul's safety and salvation (Lk19:9); in the technical biblical sense, the messianic salvation.[552] The word σώσω means: a) to save a suffering one from perishing, to make well, heal restore to health; b) in technical biblical sense it refers to deliver from the penalties of the Messianic judgment and to save from the evils which abstract the reception of Messianic deliverance.[553]

In Paul σώσω and σωτηρία are obviously limited quite intentionally to the relation between human and God. When Paul is referring to other danger from which he asks to God from deliverance and receives them from him, he uses ῥύομαι. The object of salvation is not ψυχή; it is both the whole human being and his/her πνεῦμά (1Cor 5:5).[554] Therefore, salvation is about what Christ has done in his great saving acts of sinners.[555]

550 M. Azariah, *Christ and Dalit Liberation* (Madras: Dalit Liberation Education Trust, 1985), 12-13.

551 Bailey, *Paul through Mediterranean Eyes*..., 332-333.

552 Lucient Cerfaux, *Christ in the Theology of Paul*, translated by Geoffrey Webb and Adrian Walker (New York: Herder & Herder, 1966), 12.

553 Ninian Smart, "Soteriology," *ER* 13: 418.

554 __________, *GLNT* 1:612.

555 ________, *GLNT* 1:610.

4.6.2.2 Damascus as the Turning Point

Damascus experience is very important for Paul as it is the turning point for his theological journey and especially in his understanding of soteriology.[556] Seyoon Kim says that Paul's soteriology is strongly stamped by his experience at the Damascus Christophany. The characteristics of his doctrine of justification *sola gratia* and *sola fide* are due to the insights into the questions of the law, human existence and human's relation to God which he develops out of his Damascus experience.[557]

4.6.2.3 The Role of Triune God

4.6.2.3.1 God, as the Father of Christian Salvation

It is axiomatic in Pauline soteriology that the work of Christian salvation originates with God, the Father. Paul characteristic wish for grace and peace, the summation of all the blessings of Christian salvation is from God our father.[558] Paul shows the father as the one who predestines our salvation through Christ (2Cor 13:4; Eph 1:5-7); the death of Christ as reconciliation with the Father (2Cor 5:18-19); the resurrection of Christ to bring new life as the work of the Father (1Thess 1:10); and the salvific work of Christ as the manifestation of the love of the Father (Rom 5:8-9; Eph 5:1).

4.6.2.3.2 The work of Christ as the cause of Christian Salvation

The works of the Christ, especially his death and resurrection have a significant location for the whole world history of salvation. Stanley says, "If the father is said to have handed over his son (Rom 8:32; 4:25), Christ is also said to have handed over himself to death for us" (Gal 2:20). If the Father reconciled human to himself through his son's death (2Cor 5:18; Col 1:20), Christ has accomplished their

556 Foearster, "σώσω and σωτηρία in the New Testament," *TDNT* 7: 992-993.

557 L. Morris, "Salvation," *DPL* 1:858.

558 S. J. David Michael Stanley, *Christ Resurrection in Pauline Soteriology* (Romae: E. Pontificio Instituto Biblico, 1961), 39-50.

reconciliation through his death (Rom 5:10; Eph 2:6).[559] The death of Christ has become a step in the process of salvation, which will culminate in the victory over death (1Cor 15:57). Therefore, the works of the risen Christ become the cause of Christian salvation as a transforming power for those of alive (1Cor 15:51; 1Thess 4:17) and as the transforming power into glorious resurrection for those who already dead (1Thess 4:14).

4.6.2.3.3 The Work of the Holy Spirit

While we mention of salvation primarily as the work of God, the Father and of the Christ, it will be appropriate to note that the function of the Holy Spirit in Pauline soteriology is referred chiefly to the adoptive sonship of the Christian.[560] According to James D. G Dunn, the action of the Spirit is a more prominent theme in Paul's theology of the beginning of salvation than his participation in Christ motif. It is given Spirit which determines life and living as Christian.[561] In the light of 2Cor 1:20-21 and 5:5, he says, "The Spirit is the down payment, the first installment, in other words, the beginning of the salvation process. So, also the Spirit is the (first installment, guarantee) of the process of transformation now under way in the believer, which will climax in the transformed resurrection body."[562]

4.6.2.4 Symbolism of Soteriology in Pauline writings

According to Gerd Theissen, two basic symbolic structures determine Paul's soteriology: a sociomorphic interaction symbolism (derived from the area of human social life) and a Physiomorphic transformation symbolism (derived from the realm of organic life). The later symbolic system addresses not

559 Seyoon Kim, *The Origin of Paul's Gospel* (Cambridge: William B. Eerdmans Publishing Company, 1982), 329.

560 Stanley, *Christ Resurrection in Pauline Soteriology,* 255.

561 Stanley, *Christ Resurrection in Pauline Soteriology*, 268.

562 Stanley, *Christ Resurrection in Pauline Soteriology*, 279.

personal relations-like the former-but biological and ontological structures.[563]

4.6.2.4.1 Sociomorphic Interaction Symbolism

4.6.2.4.1.1 The Symbolism of Liberation

In liberation symbolism, images of social power predominated. Salvation takes place as liberation; bondage and suppression represent the unredeemed state. The enslaving powers are Satan, death, sin, and the law. Redemption is portrayed as a change in power structures, in which the dominant position is under. The transfer from slavery to freedom (Rom 8:21) or sonship (Rom 8:15) is described by the Christological images of exaltation and ransom redemption. In other words liberation takes place either by defeat of the power or by liberation of slave from a hostile power.

4.6.2.4.1.2 The Symbolism of Justification

Justification is legal metaphor; to be justified is to be acquitted.[564] It deals with the problem of guilt. The unredeemed state is represented by people failure to obey the law, and their redemption consists in acquittal/discharge of a merited death sentence before the divine judge. People are lost because they live under the curse of the law, that is, under its condemning, deceiving and killing character. Within this 'transfer terminology' is often defined by the preposition "on behalf of" Christ's death is for us because he takes upon himself the curse of the law and expiates its punishment because of our transgression. Christ also abolishes the law and grant freedom from its (Rom 10:4).

In this context the phrase "on behalf" interchanges with clause "in order that," (cf. Gal 3:13-14; 2 Cor 5:21). However, resurrection formulas do not occur in this symbolism, because God's justification in the death of Christ is primarily a sacrificial expiation.

563 James D.G. Dunn, *The Theology of Paul the Apostle* (Grand Rapids: William B. Eerdmans Publishing Company, 1998), 328.

564 Dunn, *The Theology of Paul the Apostle*, 421.

4.6.2.4.1.3 The Symbolism of Reconciliation

It stresses the contrast between enmity and peace, hate and love (cf. Rom 5:1-12; 2Cor 5:14-21). Here the two parties at enmity are brought together into a new peace and corporation.[565] Whereas the liberation and justification symbolism function in vertical categories, reconciliation symbolism operates on a horizontal plane. Cosmic powers are hostile because they separate God and human beings (Rom 8:35-39). Redemption comes to speech as access and the death of Christ is portrayed as manifestation of love (Gal 2:20; Rom 5:8; 2Cor 5:14) and the resurrection of Christ as a beginning of new life (Rom 4:25; 8:34; 2 Cor 5:15).

4.6.2.4.2 Organic Transformation Symbolism

Here the change takes place not in personal relations but in biological structures. This organic creates hermeneutical difficulties for our understanding because the focus is on a transformation of being rather than on a change in interpersonal relationship. It also contains three basic metaphors as follows.[566]

4.6.2.4.2.1 The Symbolism of Physical (Physiomorphic) Transformation

The key terms are "image," "form," and "glory." The being of the redeemer transforms the being of the redeemed into his image or likeness as Paul says, "All of us... are being transformed into the same image from one degree of glory to another" (2Cor 3:18).

4.6.2.4.2.2 The Symbolism of Death and Life

It involves a bio-and physiomorphic symbolism like "to be united with him" (Rom 6:5); "the sharing of his suffering... in his death" (Phil 3:10). The redeemer has here an "assimilating" power; his destiny is that of the redeemed. The basic theme is victory over human finitude, which is the longing for a new creation. Whereas

565 J. Christian Baker, *Paul the Apostle: The Triumph of God I Life and Thought* (Philadelphia: Fortress Press, 1980), 256-272.

566 Dunn, *The Theology of Paul the Apostle*, 328.

in physiomorphic transformation symbolism dying is not a pre-requisite for transformation (1Cor 15:51), in death and life symbolism the total identification with the death and life of the redeemer is the condition for our participation in him.

4.6.2.4.2.3 The Symbolism of Unification

It emphasizes the victory over separation and human isolation. "Union" comes to speech in image of sexual intercourse and eating; a key term is "to be join" (1Cor 6:16-17). Erotic metaphors express the human desire to overcome the limitation of the self, whereas eating suggests the union of one body with other bodies. The symbolism appears especially in the motif of the "one" and that of "the body" (cf. Gal 2:20; 1Cor 12:12-27).

4.6.2.4.3 Other Symbolism of Salvation

4.6.2.4.3.1 The Symbolism of Redemption

It emphasizes the buying back of the slave or a war captive. The price was the redemptive price, whereby slaves were transferred from one owner to another.[567] A slave is freed when he/she is bought for another master, or when he/she can himself/herself pay the price of his/her liberty;[568] so also the slaves of the law are purchased by the work of Jesus to be set free from the burden of the law and to become the new community in Christ. Therefore, it is clear that the redemption is for Paul redemption from sin and form its consequences-death (cf. Rom 3:6-7).

4.6.2.4.3.2 The Symbolism of Sonship

Our redemption from the law means positively our adoption as sons of God. The purpose of God is sending his son into the world is to grant us his Sonship. God grants us Sonship on the basis of his redemptive work in Christ and sends the spirit of his son into our hearts; then we can call him "Abba! Father." We become sons of God as by faith and baptism we put our life on Christ

567 Dunn, *The Theology of Paul the Apostle*, 328.

568 Baker, *Paul the Apostle…*, 256-258.

and are incorporated into Christ.[569] Therefore, Paul says, "So, you are no longer a slave but a child, and if a child then also an heir, through God" (Gal 4:7). He does not stop there, but he continues to say that the believer will be conformed into the image of his Son (Rom 8:29).

4.6.2.4.3.3 The Symbolism of Transformation

Since Paul can see the first-fruits of our eschatological glorification and transformation already in our call and justification, he can actually speak of our glorification and transformation as present process progressing towards the eschatological consumption.[570] He says, "And all of us, with unveiled faces, seeing the glory of the Lord as though reflected in a mirror, are being transformed into the same image from one degree of glory to another; for this comes from the Lord, the Spirit" (2Cor 3:18).[571]

4.6.2.4.3.4 Atonement

Paul uses this term in sacrificial term. The idea of sacrifice speaks vividly and powerfully to people about the divine-human relationship. In the light of the Jewish practice of sacrifice we can note down the following four points: 1) as Jews offered sacrifice in order to make atonement for sin (Lev 1:4; 4-5), Paul see the death of Jesus as such a sacrifice dealing with sin and bringing forgiveness. 2) in the light of laying hand on the sacrificial lamb as the worshiper's sin being transferred to the unblemished sacrificial animal, Paul sees that as the sinner's sin was transferred to the spotless sacrifice, so the spotless life of the sacrifice was transferred to the sinner (Gal 3:13). 3) Paul, using propitiation in Rom 3:25 makes out Jesus'death as a sacrifice taking away the wrath of God. 4) Paul thinks what was once symbolized in

569 Dunn, *The Theology of Paul the Apostle*, 227-228.

570 Cerfaux, *Christ in the Theology of Paul…*, 134.

571 Kim, *The Origin of Paul's Gospel*, 315-316.

the Day of Atonement ritual (Lev 16) is now realized in Christ crucified.[572]

4.6.2.4.3.5 The Symbolism of New Creation

The old man refers to the Adamitic humanity whichbears the ignoble/shameful image of the man of dust, and new man refers to the new humanity which has the image of God restored to it, i.e. which is conformed to the glorious image of Christ, the last Adam.[573]As we are the transferred from solidarity with the first Adam to that with the last Adam, we become no creature to whom the divine image and glory are restored.[574]

Paul also uses the business metaphor the ἀρραβών - first instalment, guarantee (Eph 1:14) that is what the spirit is for Paul, the first instalment of the wholeness of salvation. His agriculture metaphor the ἀπαρχή, - first-fruit (Rom 11:16) refers to the gift of the spirit that is the first phase of the harvest which consists in the resurrection of the body.[575]

4.7 Salvation and Grace

Paul gives to *solo deo* (by God alone) and *sola gratia* (by Grace alone) a fundamentally new and all-comprehensive meaning.[576] Grace underscores the character of Christ event as a radically new gift that negates the old older. It signifies the complete reversal from life under the wrath of God and the power of the sin to the new life of freedom and open to access to God (Rom 5:2). The language of the grace has a special function in Paul; it reinforces and supplements the unilateral character of God's righteousness and justifying act in the death and resurrection of Christ. It marks

572 Kim, *The Origin of Paul's Gospel*, 321.

573 Dunn, *The Theology of Paul the Apostle*, 468.

574 David Wenham, *Paul: Follower of Jesus of Founder of Christianity?* (Grand Rapids/Cambridge: William B. Eerdmans Publishing Company, 1995), 150-152.

575 Kim, *The Origin of Paul's Gospel*, 322.

576 Kim, *The Origin of Paul's Gospel*, 326.

a new epoch and a new domination of power that is antithetical to that of the power of sin (Rom 520-21).[577]

4.8 Who will be Saved?

A number of Pauline texts have been thought to point towards universalism. Other Pauline texts speak of some perishing and have a particularistic understating of salvation restricted to the elect or believers.[578] For instance Rom 5:12-21 probably offers the greatest potential support for universalism as he says that through the righteous act and the obedience act of the one many will be justified and made righteous. On the other hand, "who is the savior of all people, especially of those who believe" (1Tim 4:10) refers to particular salvation. I. M Gundry-Volf says that those who see some ground for universalism in Paul have wrestled with the problem of Paul's consistency. Though some metaphors have a corporate dimension and a strong emphasis on God's gracious action, M.D. Baker and C.C. Le Bruyns say that, "Paul states the centrality of personal behalf or faith. Jesus' faithful obedience does not automatically cause all to be included in the people of God; each person must believe or trust in Jesus' faithful obedience as being what brings him or her into God's family (Rom 9:10; Gal 2:16)."[579]

4.9 The Process of Salvation

Fundamental to Paul's conception of the process of salvation, therefore, is his conviction that the believers has not yet arrived, is not yet perfect, and is always in via, in transit. It is this which determines the experience of being saved as a process of "eschatological tension"- the tension between a work begun and But not complete, between fulfillment and consummation, between a decisive "already" and a still to be worked out "not yet." Paul's gospel was eschatological not because of what he still

577 Dunn, *The Theology of Paul the Apostle*, 469.

578 Gunther Bornkamm, *Paul*, translated by D.M.G. Stalker (New York: Harper & Row, 1971), 140.

579 Baker, *Paul the Apostle...*, 264-265.

hoped would happen, but because of what he believed had already happened.[580] According to Victor Paul Furnish,

> Nor does he mean that salvation which will be fulfilled in the future has been initiated already in the present, rather his thought at this point is genuinely dialectical. Paul sees no easy chronological continuity between past, present and future. The future is totally God's future, and it does not progress or develop from the past to the present. The salvation which is already present is not, therefore, somehow qualitatively preliminary or second rate. What is given is present in the fullness.[581]

His use of inheritance and heir conveys Pauline dialectical of present and future. The inheritance itself is still to come, but the one who is designated as an heir thereby has a new status already. In that sense the future has decisively entered the present.[582] Therefore, salvation includes the past (Christ's cross and resurrection), the present in which we are united to the redemptive work of Christ, and the future with its eschatological questions.[583]

4.9.1 Salvation in the Past

There is sense in which salvation has been already taken place. When Paul says, "In hope we are saved" (Rom 8:24) he looks back the death and resurrection of Christ and the faith, in which repentant sinners has already been saved when they came to Christ. But he also speaks of hope, referring to the future when believes will experience to the full of that salvation means. The perfect participle passive tense σεσῳσμένοι, which is used in Eph 2:5, 8-"By grace you have been saved" and the aorist tense-saved ἔσωσεν and delivered used in Tit 3:5 and Col 1:13 respectively

580 Gundhy-volf, "Universalism," *DPL* 1: 956.

581 M.D Bekar and C.C. Le Bruyns, "Salvation" *GDT* 1: 786.

582 Dunn, *The Theology of Paul the Apostle*, 465.

583 Victor Paul Furnish, *Theology and Ethics in Paul* (New York: Abingdon Press, 1968), 215.

indicate that the reality of salvation an accomplished fact in the past.[584]

4.9.2 Salvation Now

When Paul speaks of the gospel as "God's power for salvation for everyone who believes" (Rom 1:16), it implies that this saving power is operative and ongoing in the present (1Cor 1:18; 15:2 2Cor 6:2 and 5:17). The present-ness also indicates by his use of the present participle: the word of the cross is power of God for those of us who are being saved (1Cor 1:18), and the use of present middle in 2 Corinthians 3:18 "And all of us… are being transformed into the same image from one degree of glory to another" indicates the present dimension of the salvation.[585]

4.9.3 A Future Salvation

Salvation is for Paul a future and eschatological term (1Cor5:5, Rom13:11, Phil1:8, 2:12 etc.); σώσω and σωτηρίαν refer to the last judgment in these passages. The content of the coming salvation is developed by Paul along two lines. 1) It is salvation from approaching wrath (Rom 5:9; 1Cor 3:15; 5:5 1Thess 5:9). This deliverance, as one should here render *σωτηρίαν*, takes place on the day of the Lord's judgment (2Cor 5:10). 2) The endowment with the divine glory in the last day is the positive content of the σωτηρίαν.[586]

This salvation has, as Paul speaks of it, both a negative and a positive aspect. Negatively it means human's deliverance from the bondage to the world with its transitory power whose only fruit is decay and corruption (2Cor 7:10; Rom 5:9). In its positive aspect salvation has to do with the total transformation of human's life and being by sovereign power at work in Christ, which is called

584 Furnish, *Theology and Ethics in Paul*, 126-127.

585 Cerfaux, *Christ in the Theology of Paul…*, 12-13.

586 Morris, "Salvation," 1:860-861.

the redemption of our bodies and transformation into the likeness his glorious body (Rom 8:23 and Phil 3:21).[587]

In the light of the above discussion salvation can be understood as a deliverance from the bondage of sin and its consequences, restoration of the new relationship between God and human being through the works of Christ and as a progressive transformation into perfect image of God, which has already happened in the past, but continues in the present and will come to the fulfillment in the future.Therefore, based on the concept of salvation in Pauline writings, we need to see how Indian church's context understands the concept of salvation.

4.10 Discrimination within the Church and Model of Petrine Christianity

In more recent times, the issue of the place of Dalits within the church has led to considerable conflicts. The Dalits Christians themselves claim that they are doubly discriminated against. The state declares itself to be secular and yet does not extend the scheduled caste privileges to Dalit Christians because they are Christians.[588] Within the church these same people are then discriminated against on the basis of their birth, eating habits, culture and traditions; they claim to have been ignored by Christian leaders and left out of the decision-making processes of the church itself.[589]

John C.B. Webster says some aspects of the life did not change for the vast majority lower communities which converted to Christianity in the times of mass movements. Most converts remained in their villages, in their occupations, in their familiar social and economic relationship.[590] For many of these converts the initial change in their circumstances was an increase in oppression and persecution that they experienced until the landholders

587 Furnish, *Theology and Ethics in Paul*, 126.

588 Foearster, TDNT, 7:993.

589 Furnish, *Theology and Ethics in Paul*, 122-123.

590 Robert W. Brown, *Dalits and the Church* (New Delhi: Center for Dalit/ Subaltern Studies, 2006), 35.

eventually realized that their conversion was not an initial step towards agrarian revolt.[591]

For converts, Christianity again became new *Jati,* made of fellow converts, higher caste converts and ruling Europeans. They took on a new identity, as they became part of this *Jati*, an identity that was nurtured and shaped by regular participation in the life of their new community.[592]

On the negative side, some converts experienced difficulty in maintaining links with members of their traditional *Jati* and a degree of disjunction was experienced in some communities.[593] Webster states that conversion to Christianity did not lead to a total change from the past. The caste and agrarian systems were too deeply entrenched to enable total change.[594] Converts experienced discrimination within the church itself. They are not allowed to partake in Lord's Table along with high caste converts. The old generation Christian and high caste converts do not have any marital relationship. In more recent times the church itself has been divided in the name of caste.

Coming to Petrine model of Christianity at Antioch, it is simple to say that it was a community in which believers even Peter himself participated and supported corporate identity. In recent times Galatians once again became the focus of vigorous controversy. F.C. Baur argues that early Christianity tried to break up from Judaism and marked throughout by the opposition between the Jewish particularism of Petrine Christianity and the universalism of Pauline Christianity.[595]

Therefore, we witness an example of Particularism of Petrine Christianity due to the pressure from the James party and Peter started behaves differently at Antioch. Similar type of phenomenon like particularism of Petrine Christianity we

591 Brown, *Dalits and the Church,* 35-36.

592 John C.B. Webster, *The Dalits Christians: A History* (New Delhi: ISPCK, 1994), 64.

593 Webster, *The Dalits Christians...,* 65.

594 Webster, *The Dalits Christians...*, 65-66.

595 Webster, *The Dalits Christians...*, 68-69.

experience in the context of North Indian Christianity. According to the Jewish Christians' view the Gentile Galatian converts could not claim participation in the full heritage of Israel's blessing as God-fearers; they must become full proselytes.[596] Therefore, it is evident that Petrine Model of Christianity is exited in North India where people are treated based on their birth, eating habits, ritualistic practices and traditions. Petrine model of Christianity is the representation of discrimination and subjugation of lower communities.

4.11 Religious Freedom and Christianity in India

Article 25 says all people are equally entitled to freedom of conscience and have the right to freely profess and practice and propagate religion. Upholding freedom is the utmost responsibility of the state but also the responsibility of every person. Religious freedom applies to all people, not just to Christians. Since the Reformation, several core arguments for religious freedom have become crystallized in the Christian tradition and are now widely recognized. Religious freedom for Christian churches is not only a political guideline for Christian. Rather, it arises from the Christian faith itself and is part of it nature on every level, in private, in the church, in everyday public life, in society at large and in politics.[597]

Religious freedom applies not only to a certain group of Christians, or to all Christians, but to all human, no matter what they believe or do not believe.[598] What arises naturally is an automatic separation of church and state in which most of people are caught up. However, state has to guarantee peace and justice for all its citizens, no matter what they believe.[599] The state is to

596 Webster, *The Dalits Christians...*, 70.

597 James. D.G. Dunn, *The Partings of the Ways between Christianity and Judaism* (London: SCM Press, 1991), 1-10.

598 James D.G. Dunn, *The Theology of Paul's Letter to the Galatians* (Cambridge: Cambridge University Press, 1994), 12.

599 Thomas Schirrmacher and Richard Howell, " Freedom of Religion or Belief from Biblical Perspective," in *Freedom of Belief and Christian Mission,*

protect religious freedom and is not to spread "our" religion.[600] Religious freedom includes religious freedom for one's own children.[601]

4.12 A Socio-Cultural Search for Christian Identity in Pluralistic Context

Under the patronage of BJP, RSS and VHP along with multiple fundamentalist groups have taken up the cause of the Hindu imposition of cultural nationalism, moral policing, attacks on churches and the demand of the reconversion of Muslim and Christian's minorities, particularly in the tribal and Dalit communities.[602] The states of Uttar Pradesh, Delhi, Orissa, Gujarat and Karnataka have suffered the most atrocities in the recent past. Some recent news items indicate this reality:

> RSS chief Mohan Bhagwat says 'reconversion' will continue, at a meeting in Kolkatta, supporting the controversial issue of 'reconversion' of Muslims and Christians to Hinduism. He said that the people were originally Hindus who were converted in to other faith and are now being brought back home '*gharvapsi*'[603] which is not conversion. He proposed that the parliament should stop the debate but bring laws against conversion.[604]

---

eds. Hans Aage Gravaas, Christof Sauer, Tormod Engelsviken, Maqsood Kamil and Knud Jorgensen (Oxford: Regnum Books International, 2015), 22-23.

600 Schirrmacher, "Freedom of Religion or Belief from Biblical Perspective…, 22.

601 Schirrmacher, "Freedom of Religion or Belief from Biblical Perspective…, 24.

602 Schirrmacher, "Freedom of Religion or Belief from Biblical Perspective…, 28.

603 Schirrmacher, "Freedom of Religion or Belief from Biblical Perspective…, 29.

604 Siga Arles, "Religious Polarization in a Hindu Context," in *Freedom of Belief and Christian Mission*, eds. Hans Aage Gravaas, Christof Sauer, Tormod Engelsviken, Maqsood Kamil and Knud Jorgensen (Oxford: Regnum Books International, 2015), 326.

Christian identity on the whole carries the label of foreignness in the minds of the people because of its association with colonialism.[605] One general assumption is that the church/ Christian identity in India in its organization, architecture, worship, creeds, confessions and doctrinal statements are no different from the church in the west.[606] The church/Christian identity is criticized as being alien in its environment because the form, the creeds and the confessions of the institutional church are alien to the Indian philosophical, religious and socio-cultural traditions.[607]

Various attempts have been made by the different theologians and biblical scholars who tried to redefine Christian identity in India. M.M Thomas, A.P. Nirmal, Lesslie Newbigin, Robin Boyd and Romila Thaper are few names for that. In the most recent times, the challenge in front of Christianity in India is that what types of Christianity they need to presents or who is the role model for Christian identity? Looking at the present scenario, it is difficult to follow and present alien Christianity and its tradition in the pluralistic context. We need an accommodative identity that could provide space for all irrespective of their birth, caste, tradition and above the concept of purity and pollution.

4.13 The Story and Doctrine of Lord's Supper: An Archetype for Christian Identity

The Jewish gathering was on the basis of racc and the Roman gathering was on the basis of profession. The Christian gathering was based upon the declaration that in Christ there is neither Jews nor Greek, male or female, rich nor poor, master nor slave.[608] The central aspect of the Supper is praise that relates to a story of feast. There are two major roots to the story of the Supper. One

605 In North India Particularly many Christians have been forced to accept the Ideology of Hindusim. It is an act of Back to Hinduism.

606 *Deccan Herald*, 21st December 2014, 1.

607 Dhirendra Kumar Sahu, *The Church of North India: A Historical and Systematic Theological Inquiry into an Ecumenical Ecclesiology* (New York: Peter Lang, 1992), 179.

608 Sahu, *The Church of North India...*, 179.

was Jesus' table-fellowship and second was the meal which Jews celebrated, and still celebrate each year at the Passover.[609] The table-fellowship and Lord's Supper is an expression of friendship and hospitality.[610] Nevertheless, one failure on the part of the church is to treat the supper as just a matter of individual piety rather than a corporate community celebration in anticipation of a meal in the kingdom. The perpetuation of individual piety in a caste society like India becomes again a barrier to communion where eating together with outcaste is still a problem.[611]

Thereby, the Lord's Supper is a challenge to the church when it remains static and unquestioning with regard to injustice within the life of the community. It may play a role of an Archetype for Christian Identity through that all may be one. India is not by tradition individualist[612] but if we remain same state of injustice and do not allow our past baggage to set apart, the days are not far away when India would be an individualistic state in which family and community would not be having any role to play. To sum up, Lord's Supper and table-fellowship open the door for all to be one and unite under the umbrella of new Christian identity in which high caste and lower caste Christians could enjoy the eternal fellowship.

4.14 Best Example for Christian Identity in India: Paul or Peter

Particularism of Petrine Christianity and universalism of Pauline Christianity could be the deciding factors for the best example for Christian identity in India. However, both model of Christianity have been practiced and existed in the Indian Christian tradition throughout the country. Particularly in north India, particularism

609 Sahu, *The Church of North India...*, 179-180.

610 Dhirendra Kumar Sahu, *The Church of North India: A Historical and Systematic Theological Inquiry into an Ecumenical Ecclesiology* (New York: Peter Lang, 1992), 295.

611 Timothy Gorringe, *Redeeming Time* (London: DLT, 1986), 150-174.

612 James D.G. Dunn, Whatever Happened to the Lord's Supper? *Epworth Review*. Vol. IX, No. 1 (January, 1992): 35.

of Petrine Christianity could not be suitable model because it has various indifferences based on rituals, customs, purity and pollution etc. Converts in north India already are the victims of casteism, untouchability, discrimination in Lord's Supper, problems with the getting together of high and lower caste people in the church and society and various eating habits that are related to religious sentiment and culture of the community.

Paul defended his belief that there is no distinction between Jews and Gentiles by appealing precisely to the unity of God and His impartiality. He had to explain the purpose of God which could encompass the crucified Messiah. But he had to struggle with the dialectical tension between Israel's past and future place in God's purpose. In the words of Krister Stenhahl, Paul has often seen through the lenses of Luther or Augustine, but in he was a successful Jews (Phil 3:2). Therefore, Stendahl argued that the problem of late medieval piety cannot be read back into first century.[613] Thus, image of the Body of Christ is predominantly Pauline and therefore, the one who is chosen for many, and therefore, interpersonal relatedness belongs to the very being of God and there can be no salvation for human except in relatedness.[614] To sum up, Pauline model of Christianity could be a suitable approach to the North Indian Context in which all people can accommodate themselves irrespective of their indifferences.

4.15 Implications

Plurality is understood as the presence of two or more states or principles which co-exist together and this term has been widely used to refer to the religious pluralism that prevails in India.[615] Plurality is not a novel happening to the present context.[616] There have always been different pluralities prevailing in the

613 Sahu, *The Church of North India…*, 299.

614 Sahu, *The Church of North India…*, 310.

615 Krister Stendahl, *Paul among Jews and Gentiles* (London: SCM Press, 1977), 5.

616 Geoffrey Wainwright, ed. *Keeping the Faith* (London: SPCK, 1989), 339.

world.[617] The church has been portrayed as the institution which is responsible to be a Christian witness to the world.[618]

In a context where there are many religions, the role of the church is very important. The outlook of the church towards other religions plays a deciding role, as it can create both positive and negative effects towards different religious community. The Church has gone through different paradigm shifts in its effort to address pluralistic context. The idea of exclusivism was its stand for a long time which proposes that there can be no salvation apart from Christianity.[619] In this view there is a failure of the church to recognize the truth and saving power in other religions.[620]

Therefore, to redefine the Christian Identity for India pluralistic context, universalism of Pauline Christianity model fits in and helps the Indian context. For this there are several reasons can be given: (1) Paul advocates social justice for all, (2) Paul presents God as creator and sustainer of all life, (3) Paul offers eschatological hope and peace for all in Christ Jesus and (4) he negates the notion of discrimination. Moreover, Pauline model of Christianity is relevant and suitable model for Indian Christian identity. Thus, we believe in oneness, unity, and diversity of our faith.

Summary

Religious pluralism, caste system, nationalism, and cultural gapes define religious identity in India or we can say these are the deciding factors behind the individual's identity. Secondly, how persecution of minorities has been increased in the recent past

617 O.V. Jathanna, "Religious Pluralism: A Theological Critique," *Bangalore Theological Forum* XXXI/2 (December, 1999): 2.

618 Ignatius Puthiadam, "Theology of Religions in Indian Context," *Religious Pluralism: An Indian Christian Perspective*, 191-228.

619 M.M. Thomas, *Risking Christ for Christ's Sake: Towards an Ecumenical Theology of Pluralism* (Geneva: WCC Publications, 1987), 1.

620 Matthew Vekathanam, "Source of Jewish- Christian Specificity Claims," *Religious Pluralism: An Introduction to Christian Perspective,* edited by Kuncheria Pathil (Delhi: ISPCK, 1999), 35.

because of certain cultural habits of individual and community: for example, eating habits are closed associated with the identity. Thirdly, how Paul and Peter could be the two representations of two different models for Indian Christianity and what could be the socio-cultural approach in pluralistic context. The model of Pauline Christianity could be adopted and suggested for the India Context for two reasons; (1) Paul's model of Christianity is accommodative for all; (2) it serves the purpose of the national integrity. However, it has been noticed that many church and individual follow Petrine model of Christianity due to their own interest and profits.

The words grace, gift, and faith play an important role in the theology of salvation in Pauline writings. Salvation is a gift from God alone, and faith is a faithful response from human being to the gracious gift of God to become a member of covenantal community. It is also obvious that the doctrine of salvation is articulated not only in vertical way but also in horizontal way in Pauline writings. It is essential that the understanding of salvation in vertical way should be in equilibrium with horizontal way of salvation. The ethical implications of the eschatological aspect of salvation in Pauline writings should be expressed in an effective way in the present context.

The dimensions of universal and particular salvation presented in the symbolism of salvation in Pauline writings can be easily misunderstood without proper in-depth study. From the light of the above discussion we can assert that Christ works out salvation for all people; this does not mean that all the people will be saved, but rather those who believe in him will be saved.

However, Soteriology is an important theological theme in Pauline writings as the foundation for the Christian understanding of salvation has been formulated in a proper sense. It would be one of the important key words to understand the theology of Pauline writings.

Chapter 5

General Conclusion

This research is an attempt to explain and explore the Paul's confrontation with Peter in Antioch and after interpreting the Galatians 2; 11-21 how one can best redefine the Christian identity in pluralistic context. In Gal 2:11-21 Paul responds to the Antiochan, in which divisions were created between Jews and gentiles because of Peter's withdrawal from the table fellowship with the Gentiles. By confronting Peter, Paul clearly advocates that the church is a corporate, organized and functional entity, which exists as community of all people. It is clear from Paul's response to the issue that his theological articulation focuses on the communitarian reality of the church.

Throughout his entire confrontation with Peter, the ultimate purpose is on togetherness of all believers' community rather than individual's existence. Moreover, it is evident from the study that Paul's confrontation is a dialogical conformation and socio-religious dialogue incorporates some type of confrontation that depends on truth.

The exegetical analysis of the text highlights briefly the background of the Antiochan incident and provides reason for Paul astonishment. Paul justifies and exposes Peter's attitude which was a hypocritical act because Peter negates the truth of the gospel for which he was commissioned by Jesus himself. The exegetical analysis digs out the historical, theological and cultural aspects of the text that helps to understand the intensity of Paul's confrontation of Peter.

Paul's Christological and missiological framework gives new directions to understand his mission to Gentiles. Paul presents Jesus Christ as messiah for all whose divinity and humanity inaugurates a spiritual kingdom in which salvation comes by faith not by the works of Law. Paul's mission to Gentiles replaces supplements and completes the mission to Israel.

Some of Christians have witnessed tragic and unforgettable memories since its emergence both within and outside the church. Purification of these memories is not at all easy. People and religious communities cannot be asked to forget how much they have suffered, even at the hand of some notorious Christians. For the people and communities forgetting would be tantamount of betrayal.[621]

The personal identity of a human group is built up from a concrete historic past that in any case cannot be annulled, even if there were a will to do so. But even while not forgetting, memory can be healed and purified through a shared determination to begin new constructive mutual relations to dialogue and collaboration, of encounter.[622] After becoming first an accepted religion in Roman Empire Christianity developed an exclusivist attitude combined with a negative assessment of other religions. The church was considered the only "ark of salvation"- outside of it human beings were lost.[623] Christianity still has kept this type of notion, like Jewish people thought they are chosen one, for others. Today

621 Gravin D' Costa, *Theology and Religious Pluralism: The Challenge of other Religions* (Oxford: Basil Blackwell, 1986), 52.

622 Paul F. Kntter, *One Earth Many Religions: Multi-Faith Dialogue and Global Responsibility* (New York: Orbit Books, 1995), 26-27.

623 Jacques Dupuis, S.J., *Christianity and the Religions: From Confrontation to Dialogue* (New York: Orbis Books, 2003), 5.

there is need along with the purification of memories, theological language and interpretations also need to be purified.

While speaking clearly of a "new covenant" (2Cor 3:6; Heb 9:15; 12:14) and of the church as "people of God" (1Pet 2:9-11), the New Testament never uses the expression "new People of God" for the church.[624] Does such an identification, which at least implicitly excludes "others" from the Reign of God, fit with the thought of the Historic Jesus? In reality, the New Testament is not about the people of God being replaced by another, but about the expansion of the people of God beyond its own limits through the extension of the church which now part of it, to all the nations. Therefore, Paul advocates an accommodative place for all within and outside the church. He proposes that Christian identity is based on faith not based on merit or works.

Today's multiethnic, multicultural and multi-religious world requires from all parts a qualitative leap that is encounter with each other through dialogue and collaboration and requires some kinds of confrontation so that justice and truth may rule. To be more specific, a cultural component that has been imbibed by a community in its inherited pole would have its counterpart in the acquired pole. In such a situation, that particular experience would not be complete only with either of these poles. Rather, the experiences of both poles have to be taken as a whole. Consider the food habits of a person living in an urban area, who is originally from a rural sector. In the rural/inherited pole, he/she would like to have the traditional food items to which he/she was used to.

At the same time, the urban/acquired pole would like to have the taste of urban specials. The taste is an assemblage of both the rural and the urban, in which a constant crossing over and coming back of rural and urban occurs concurrently.This transcending of cultural experiences is termed as transculturalism.

Indian Christians having their lineage to and interactions with diverse cultural groups undergo transcultural experience. Predominantly belonging to the Dalit, Tribal, General and OBC groups, their cultural experiences are largely multiple and fluid.

624 Dupuis, *Christianity and the Religions...*, 5.

Intersectionalities of their cultural experiences have revealed their fivefold trans-experience such as trans-ethnic, trans-lingual, trans-regional and trans-denominational.

Recognition of the cultural experience of the Indian Christians as transcultural, leads towards a reconsideration of the role of culture (here transculturalism) in constructing theo/christology. Here, Paul's and Galatians' experiences are the starting point of theo/christology. The cultural experience of the Indian Christians reveals the dipolarity of their experience that has a pole of 'broken experiences' consisting of brokenness, marginality or depravity as well as a pole of 'privileged experiences' with information, celebration, self-esteem, influence, authority etc.

According to Goldie Osuri, "everyone knows that the great majority of Indian Christians ate meat and drank liquor before they became Christians,"[625] still they continue. However, eating pork and beef together in certain context of India is a question of socio-religious harmony. This habit of eating both meats creates problems in Christianity and this is a hurdle and stumbling block for many. Based on eating habits we find discrimination within Christianity itself.

To sum up, Pauline model of Christianity serve as the best model for Christian identity in India because Paul presents the concept of identity in two ways: the community which belongs to a table-fellowship that is based on the Jewish Torah and second community which belongs to Jesus as Messiah irrespective of differences. Paul says, what matters is not now Torah, but Messiah.

Justification is all about being declared to be a member of God's people; and this people are defined in relation to the Messiah himself. The Messiah is not, as it were, simply a fixed point around which the people must regroup. The manner of the messiah's fulfillment of his task, i.e. his death and resurrection, must from the central characteristic of his people. The cross and resurrection thus provide the fresh shaping of our identity. If Jesus

625 Dupuis, *Christianity and the Religions...*, 6.

is indeed our Messiah, then we should be formed according to the pattern of his death and resurrection.

New Testament scholarship has dealt with this topic from various point of views, however, the present study has shed some light, though not exhaustively, towards interpreting and redefining the Christian identity in pluralistic context from the passage on table-fellowship or eating together in the authentic Pauline letter. Therefore, this study could be an opening for the further investigation on this subject.

Bibliography

A. Text and Translations

Allan, Barbara, et. al., eds. *The Greek New Testament.* 4th rev. ed. Stuttgart: United Bible Societies, 1994.

The Holy Bible. *New Revised Standard Version.* Grand Rapids: Zondervan, 1989.

B. Dictionaries, Commentaries, Books and Book Sections

Arles, Siga "Religious Polarization in a Hindu Context," in *Freedom of Belief and Christian Mission*, eds. Hans Aage Gravaas, Christ of Sauer, Tormod Engelsviken, Maqsood Kamil and Knud Jorgensen. Oxford: Regnum Books International, 2015.

Asano, and Atsuhiro. *Community-Identity Construction in Galatians: Exegetical, Social-Anthropological and Socio-Historical Studies.* Sheffield: Sheffield Academic Press, 2005.

Azariah, M. *Christ and Dalit Liberation.* Madras: Dalit Liberation Education Trust, 1985.

__________. *Christ and Dalit Liberation.* Madras: Dalit Liberation Education Trust, 1985.

Azariah, M. *The Un-Christian Side of the Indian Church.* Bangalore: Dalit Sahitya Akademy, 1985.

Bailey, Kenneth E. *Paul through Mediterranean Eyes: Cultural Studies in 1 Corinthians.* Illinois: IVP Academic, 2011.

Baker, J. Christian. *Paul the Apostle: The Triumph of God I Life and Thought*. Philadelphia: Fortress Press, 1980, 256-272.

Baker, J. Christian. *The Triumph of God: The Essence of Paul's Thought,* translated by Loren T. Stuckenbruck. Minneapolis: Augsburg Fortress, 1990.

Balasuriya, Tissa. *The Eucharist and Human Liberation*. London: SCM, 1977), 18-20; N.T. Wright, *Jesus and the Victory of God* Minneapolis: Fortress Press, 1996.

Banks, Robert. *Paul's Idea of Community*. Massachusetts: Hendrickson Publishers, Inc, 1994.

Barclay, John M. G. "'Neither Jew nor Greek': Multiculturalism and the New Perspective on Paul," in *Ethnicity and the Bible*. ed. Mark G. Brett; New York: E. J. Brill Publishers, 1996.

Barclay, John. *Obeying the Truth: A Study of Paul's Ethics in Galatians*. Edinburgh: T&T Clark, 1988.

Barrett, C.K. *Freedom and Obligation: A Study of the Epistle to the Galatians*. London: SPCK, 1985.

__________. *Essay on Paul*. Philadelphia: The Westminster Press, 1962.

Bartlett, John R. *Jews in the Hellenistic World*. London: Cambridge University Press, 1985.

Barton, John. *Oracles of God: Perceptions of Ancient Prophecy in Israel after the Exile*. London: Darton, Longman and Todd, 1986.

Bassler, Jouette M. *Navigating Paul: An Introduction to Key Theological Concepts*. Louisville: Westminster John Knox Press, 2007.

Bauer, Walter, et al. *A Greek-English Lexicon of the New Testament and Other Early Christian Literature*. trans. by William F. Arndt and F. Wilbur Gingrich, 2nd ed. Chicago: The University of Chicago Press, 1979.

Baur, F.C. *Paul: His Life and Works*. London: Williams & Norgate, 1873.

Beale, G.K. "Eschatology" in *Dictionary of the Later New Testament and its Development,* edited by Ralph Martin and Peter David. Leicester: InterVarsity Press, 1997.

Benjamin, Jerry D. *For Freedom: Studies on Galatians*. Franklin, Tennessee: Providence House.

Berger, P.L. and T. Luckmann, *The Social Construction of Reality*. London: Penguin, 1967. Publishers, 1993.

Betz, Hans Dieter. *Galatians: A Commentary on Paul's Letter to the Churches in Galatia.* Philadelphia: Fortress Press, 1979.

__________. "Epistles to the Galatians." in *Anchor Bible Dictionary*, 872-75, Edited by D. Freedman. 6 vols. New York: Doubleday, 1992.

Blair, P.A. "Gentiles," in *NBD*, 3rd ed. Secunderabad: OM Books, 2000.

Blair, Joe. *Introducing the New Testament.* Nashville, Tennessee: Broadmen and Holman Publishers, 1994.

Blenkinsopp, Joseph *Sage. Priest, Prophet: Religious and Intellectual Leadership in Ancient Israel.* Louisville: Westminster/John Knox Press, 1995.

Bornkamm, Gunter. *Paul,* translated by D.M.G. Stalker. New York: Harper & Row, Publishers, 1969.

Boyarin, Daniel. *A Radical Jews: Paul and the Politics of Identity*. Los Angeles: University of California Press, 1994.

Brown, Robert W. *Dalits and the Church*. New Delhi: Center for Dalit/Subaltern Studies, 2006.

Bruce, F.F. *The International Greek Testament Commentary on Galatians.* Michigan: William B. Eerdmans Publishing Company, 1982.

__________. *Paul: Apostle of the Heart Set Free*. Michigan: William B. Eerdmans Publishing Company, 1979.

__________. Galatians: NIGTC. Michigan: William B. Eerdmans Publishing Company, 1982.

Brueggemann, Walter. *Theology of the Old Testament: Testimony, Dispute, Advocacy*. Minneapolis: Fortress Press, 1997.

Burton, Ernest De. Witt *A Critical and Exegetical Commentary on the Epistles to the Galatians*. Edinburg: T&T Clark, 1964.

Capes, D.B. *Old Testament Yahweh Texts in Paul's Christology*. Tubingen: Mohr-Siebeck, 1992.

Carl, K. James. *The Pauline view of Christian Freedom*. Madras: The United Evangelical Lutheran Church, 1999.

__________. *The Epistle to the Galatians: A Commentary on the Greek Text.* Exeter: Patersonster Press, 1982.

Cerfaux, Lucient. *Christ in the Theology of Paul*, translated by Geoffrey Webb and Adrian Walker. New York: Herder & Herder, 1966.

Charles, R.H. ed. *The Apocrypha and Pseudepigrapha of the Old Testament in English*. Oxford: The Clarendon Press, 1964.

Charlesworth, James H. ed. *The Old Testament Pseudepigrapha,* Vol. 2. New York: 1985.

Cooper, Stephen. *Marius Victorinus, Commentary on Galatians*. New York: Oxford University Press, 2005.

Cullmann, Oscar. *Peter: Disciple, Apostle, Martyr.* Philadelphia: Westminster/John Knox Press, 1962.

D'Costa, Gravin. *Theology and Religious Pluralism: The Challenge of other Religions.* Oxford: Basil Blackwell, 1986.

Deissmann, G.A. *Paul: A Study in Social and Religious History*, 2nd ed. London: Hodder & Stoughton, 1926.

Dhillon, Dalbir Singh. *Sikhism: Origin and Development.* New Delhi: Atlantic Publishers & Distributers, 1988.

Donaldson, Terence. *Paul and Gentiles: Remapping the Apostle's Convictional World.* Minneapolis: Fortress Press, 1997.

Dunn, James D.G. *Jesus, Paul and the Law*. London: SPCK, 1990.

__________. *The Theology of Paul's Letter to the Galatians*. Cambridge: Cambridge University Press, 1994.

__________. *Theology of Paul the Apostle*. Michigan: William B. Eerdmans Publishing Company, 1998.

__________. *Christology in the Making*. Grand Rapids: Eerdmans, 1996.

__________. *The Partings of the Ways between Christianity and Judaism*. London: SCM Press, 1991.

Dunn, James D.G. *The New Perspective on Paul the Apostle*. Grand Rapids: William B. Eerdmans Publishing Company, 2005.

Dunn, James D.G. *The Theology of Paul the Apostle*. Grand Rapids: William B. Eerdmans Publishing Company, 1998.

Dunn, James D.G. *The Theology of Paul's Letter to the Galatians*. Cambridge: Cambridge University Press, 1994.

Dupuis, Jacques S.J., *Christianity and the Religions: From Confrontation to Dialogue*. New York: Orbis Books, 2003.

Ebeling, G. *the Truth of the Gospel: An Exposition of Galatians*. Trans. By David Green; Philadelphia: Fortress, 1988.

Elliott, John H. *What is Social-Scientific Criticism?* Minneapolis, MN: Fortress Press, 1993.

__________. *A Home for the Homeless: A Sociological Exegesis of 1 Peter, Its Situation and Strategy*. Philadelphia, PA: Fortress Press, 1981.

Elliott, Susan. *Cutting Too Close for Comfort: Paul's Letter to the Galatians in its Anatolian Cultic Context*. New York: T&T Clark International, 2003.

Enslin, Orton Scott. *The Ethics of Paul*. New York: Harper and Brothers, 1930.

Esler, P.P. *Galatians*. London and New York: Routledge, 1998.

Esler, Philip F. "Group Boundaries and Intergroup Conflict in Galatians: A New Reading of Galatians 5:13–6:10," in *Ethnicity and the Bible*. ed. Mark G. Brett; New York: E. J. Brill Publishers, 1996.

__________. *Community and Gospel in Luke-Acts: The Social and Political Motivations of Lucan Theology*. Cambridge: Cambridge University Press, 1978.

__________. *New Testament Theology: Communion and Community*. Minneapolis, MN: Fortress Press, 2005.

Fitzmyer, S.J. Joseph A. The Letter to the Galatians: NJBC, edited by Raymond E. Brown., Banglore: TBI, 2000.

Fitzmyer, Joseph A. *Pauline Theology: A Brief Sketch*. New Jersey: Prentice Hall, Inc., 1967.

Fowler, Jeaneane D. *Hinduism: Beliefs and Practices*. Oregon: Sussex Academic Press, 1997.

Frykenberg, Robert Eric. "Gospel, Globalization and Hindutva: The Policies of Conversion in India," in *Christianity Reborn: The Global Expansion of Evangelism in the Twentieth Century*, edited by Donald M. Lewis. Grand Rapids: William B. Eerdmans Publishing Company, 2004.

Fung, Y. K. Ronald. The Epistle to the Galatians, Michigan: William B. Eerdmans Publishing Company, 1988.

Furnish, Victor Paul. *Theology and Ethics in Paul*. New York: Abingdon Press, 1968.

Gardner, P.D. *The Gifts of God and the Authentication of a Christian: An Exegetical Study of 1 Corinthians 8-11:1*. Lanham, New York, London: University Press of America, 1994.

Gasque, W.W. *A History of the Criticism of the Acts of the Apostles*. Grand Rapids: William B. Eerdmans Publishing Company, 1975.

Gaston, Lloyd. "Paul and the Torah," in *Antisemitism and the Foundations of Christianity,* edited by Alan T. Davies. New York: Pauhst, 1979.

George, Timothy. *Galatians*: *The New American Commentary*. Nashville: Broadman & Holmann Publishers, 1994.

Giesen, Heinz. "Eschatology in Philippians," in *Paul and His Theology,* edited by Stanley E. Porter. Leiden, Boston: Brill, 2006.

Goldstein, Jonathan. *I Maccabees,* Garden City, New York: Doubleday and Company, Inc., 1976.

Gorringe, Timothy. *Redeeming Time*. London: DLT, 1986.

Gragg, Kenneth. *Paul and Peter.* London: Bible Reading Fellowship, 1980.

Grumett, David and Rachel Muers, eds. *Eating and Believing: Interdisciplinary Perspectives on Vegetarianism and Theology*. London: T&T Clark, 2008.

Gunther. *Paul*, translated by D.M.G. Stalker. New York: Harper & Row, 1971, 140.

Guthrie, Donald. *New Testament Theology.* Illinois, Leicester: InterVarsity Press, 1981.

Hamilton, Neill Q. *The Holy Spirit and Eschatology in Paul.* London: Oliver and Boyd Ltd, 1957.

Hawthrone, Gerald F. and Ralph P. Martin, *Dictionary of Paul and His Letters*. Leicester: InterVarsity Press, 1993.

Hayes, John H. and J. Maxwell Miller, eds. *Israelite and Judean History*. Philadelphia: Trinity Press International, 1977.

Haynes, Douglas and Gyan Prakash, "Introduction: The Entanglement of Power and Resistance," in *Contesting Power: Resistance and Everyday Social Relations in South Asia,* edited by Douglas Haynes and Gyan Prakash. London/Delhi: Oxford University Press, 1991.

Hemer, Colin, *The Book of Acts in the Setting of Hellenistic History*. Edited by C. Gemf. Winona Lake, Ind.: Eisenbranus, 1990.

Hengel, M. *The Son of God.* London: SCM, 1976.

Hengel, Martin and Anna Maria Schwemer. *Paul between Damascus and Antioch* tr. By John Bowden (London: SCM Press, 1997.

Hengel, Martin. *Judaism and Hellenism*, translated by John Bowen. Philadelphia: Fortress Press, 1974.

Hietanen, Mika. *Paul's Argumentation in Galatians*. London: T&T Clark, 2007.

Holder, John. *The Intertestamental Period.* London: SPCK, 1994.

Horrell, D.G. *"The Lord's Supper at Corinth and in the Church Today,"* Theology 98 (1995): 196-202.

Horsley, Richard A. *Sociology and the Jesus Movement.* New York: Continuum, 1994.

Hultgren, Arland J. "Paul's Christology and His Mission to the Gentiles," in *Paul as Missionary: Identity, Activity, Theology and Practice*, eds. by Trevor J. Burke and Brian S. Rosner. London: T & T Claek, 2011.

Jeremias, J. *New Testament Theology*: The Proclamation of Jesus. Vol.1. London: SCM Press, 1971.

Jervell, Jacob. "Luke and People of God," in *A New Look at Luke-Acts*. Minneapolis: Augsburg Publishing House, 1972.

Kapelrud, Arvid S. *Israel: From the Earliest Time to the Birth of Christ*. Oxford: Basil Blackwell, 1966.

Kim, Seyoom. *The Origin of Paul's Gospel*. Michigan: William B. Eerdmans Publishing Company, 1981.

Kittel, Gerhard and Gerhard Friedrich, *Theological Dictionary of the New Testament*, abridged in one volume by Geoffrey W. Bromiley. Grand Rapids, Michigan: William B. Eerdmans Publishing Company, 1984.

Kntter, Paul F. *One Earth Many Religions: Multi-Faith Dialogue and Global Responsibility*. New York: Orbit Books, 1995.

L. Morris, "Salvation," *DPL* 1:858.

Lacey, D.R. De. "Gentiles," in *DPL*. Illinois: InterVarsity Press, 1993.

Ladd, George Eldon. *A Theology of the New Testament.* Michigan: William B. Eerdmans Publishing Company, 1974.

Lightfoot, J. B. *The Epistle of St. Paul to the Galatians.* Grand Rapids: Zondervan, 1965.

__________. *Saint Paul's Epistle to the Galatians*. London: Macmillan, 1892.

__________. *Saint's Paul's Epistles to the Colossians and to Philemon*. Grand Rapids: Zondervan Publishing House, 1879.

__________. *Saint Paul's Epistle to the Philippians*. Peabody MA: Hendrickson, 1993.

Lohse, Eduard "Changes of Thought in Pauline Theology? Some Reflections on Paul's Ethical Teachings in the Context of His Theology," in *Theology and Ethics in Paul and His Interpreters: Essays in Honor of Victor Paul Furnish*, Eugene H. Lovering Jr. and Jerry L. Sumney, eds. Nashville: Abingdon Press, 1996.

Longenecker, Richard N. "Galatians". *World Biblical Commentary*. Vol. 41. Dallas: Word Books Publisher, 1990.

__________. *Word Biblical Commentary,* Vol. 41: *Galatians.* (Dallas, Texas: Word Books Publisher, 1998.

__________. "The Epistle of St. Paul to Thessalonica, Galatians and Romans," *WBC* 41; Dallas, Texas: Word Books, 1998.

Longenecker, Richard N. "New Testament Social Ethics for Today," in Brian S. Rosner ed. *Understanding Paul's Ethics: Twentieth Century Approaches*. Grand Rapids, Michigan: William B. Eerdmans Publishing Company, 1995.

Lowery, David K. "A Theology of Paul's Missionary Epistles" in *A Biblical Theology of the New Testament,* edited by Roy B. Zuck. Chicago: Moody Press, 1994.

Luhrmann, Dieter. *Galatians: A Continental Commentary*. Translated by O. C. Dean Minneapolis: Fortress Press, 1992.

Macdonald, Margaret Y. *The Pauline Churches: A Socio-Historical Study of Institutionalization in the Pauline and Deutero-Pauline Writings*. Cambridge: Cambridge University Press, 1998.

Malina, Bruce. "Reading Theory Perspective: Reading Luke-Acts," in *The Social World of Luke-Acts: Models for Interpretation.* ed. Jerome Neyrey; Peabody, MA: Hendrickson, 1991.

__________. "Social Sciences and Biblical Interpretation," *The Bible and Liberation: Political and Social Hermeneutics.* rev. ed.; ed. Norman K. Gottwald; New York: Orbis Books, 1989.

__________. *New Testament World: Insights from Cultural Anthropology*. 3rd rev. ed.; Louisville, KY: Westminster John Knox Press, 2001.

__________. and John J. Pilch. *Social-Science Commentary on the Letters of Paul.* Minneapolis, MN; Fortress Press, 2006.

Maloney, George A. *The Cosmic Christ: From Paul to Teilhard.* New York: Sheed and Ward, 1968.

Manson, T.W. *On the Paul and John.*, edited by M. Black. London, _______, 1963.

__________. *Studies in the Gospels and Epistles*. Manchester: 1962.

__________. *On the Paul and John*, edited by, M. Black. London, _______, 1963.

Marshal, I.H. "Titles of Jesus Christ" in *New Bible Dictionary.* Edited by I.H. Marshal et, al. Secunderabad: OM Books, 3rd ed., 2000.

Martin, R.P. *2 Corinthians*. WBC 40; Waco, TX: Word Books, 1986.

Massey, James. *Letter of Paul to the Romans and Galatians*. New Delhi: Centre for Dalit/Subaltern Studies, 2008.

Meeks, W.A. *The First Urban Christians*: *The Social World of the Apostle Paul.* London: Yale University Press, 1983.

Michael, S.M. "Culture, Nation, Conversion: Issues for Mission," in *the Church in India in the Emerging Third Millennium*, edited by Fr. Thomas D'Sa. Bangalore: NBCLC, 2005.

Mott, S.C. "Ethics" in *Dictionary of Paul and His Letters*, edited by Gerald F. Hawthorne, Ralph P. Martin and Daniel G. Reid. Leicester: InterVarsity Press, 1993.

Moule, C.F.D. *The Origin of Christology*. Cambridge: CUP, 1977.

Nadich, Judah. *Jewish Legends of the Second Commonwealth*. Philadelphia: The Jewish Publication Society of America, 1983.

Nanos, Mark D. Ed., *The Galatians Debate*. Massachusetts: Hendrickson Publishers, 2002.

Ndiokwere, Nathaniel. *Prophecy and Revolution*. London: SPCK, 1981.

O'Brien, P.T. *The Epistle to the Philippians*. Grand Rapids: William B. Eerdmans Publishing Company, 1991.

Olivelle, Patrick. *Manu's Code of Law*. Oxford: Oxford University Press, 2005.

Osuri, Goldie. *Religious Freedom in India: Sovereignty and (anti) Conversion*. London and New York: Routledge, 2013.

Perkins, Pheme. *New Testament Introduction*. Allahabad: ST Pauls, 2002.

____________. *Abraham's Divided Children: Galatians and the Politics of Fait*h. Harrisburg: T&T Clark International.

Peterson, David L. "Eschatology," in *The Anchor Bible Dictionary,* edited by David Noel Freedman et al., Vol. 2. New York: Double Day, 1992.

Pickett, R. *The Cross in Corinth: The Social Significance of the Death of Jesus*. Sheffield: SAP, 1997.

Polhill, J.B. *New American Commentary: Acts* Vol. 26. Nashville: Broadman Press, 1992. Trinity Press International, 2001.

__________. *New Testament Introduction.* Allahabad: ST Pauls, 2002.

Prince, R. M. 'Schweitzer Albert' in *New Dictionary Theology*, edited by Sinclair B. Ferguson and David F. Wright. Leicester: InterVarsity Press, 1988.

Puthiadam, Ignatius. "Theology of Religions in Indian Context," *Religious Pluralism: An Indian Christian Perspective.*

Rajshekhar, V.J. *Weapons to Fight Counter Revolution*. Bangalore: Dalit Sahtiya Akademy, 2004.

Rengstrof, Karl H. "ἁμαρτωλός" in I. Grand Rapids: William B. Eerdmans Publishing Company, 1964.

Ridderbos, H. *Paul: The Outline of His Theology*. Grand Rapids: William B. Eerdmans Publishing Company, 1975.

Ridderbos, Herman. *Paul: An Outline of His Theology,* translated by John Richard Dewitt. Grand Rapids: William B. Eerdmans Publishing Company, 1975.

Robinson. Anthony B. and Robert W. Wall, *Called to Be Church: The Book of Acts for a New Day*. Michigan: William B. Eerdmans Publishing Company, 2006.

Ronald ,Y.K. "The Epistle to the Galatians." *The New International Commentary on the New Testament.* Michigan: William B. Eerdmans Publishing Company, 1988.

Roy, P. "conversion," in *Global Dictionary of Theology*, edited by William A. Dyrness and Veli Matti Karkkainen. Nottingham: IVP, 2008.

Sahu, Dhirendra Kumar. *The Church of North India: A Historical and Systematic Theological Inquiry into an Ecumenical Ecclesiology*. New York: Peter Lang, 1992.

Sanders, E.P. *Paul and Palestinian Judaism: A Comparison of Patterns of Religion*. Philadelphia: Fortress Press, 1977.

__________. *Paul and Palestinian Judaism*. London: SCM, 1977.

__________. *Paul, the Law and the Jewish People*. Philadelphia: Fortress Press, 1983.

Sanders, E.P. *Paul, the Law and the Jewish People.* Philadelphia: Fortress Press, 1983, 176.

Sanders, E.P. *Paul and Palestinian Judaism: A Comparison of Pattern of Religion*. London: SCM Press Ltd, 1997.

Sanders, Jack T. *Jews in Luke-Acts*. Philadelphia: Fortress Press, 1987.

Schirrmacher, Thomas and Richard Howell, "Freedom of Religion or Belief from Biblical Prespecitve," in *Freedom of Belief and Christian Mission*, eds. Hans Aage Gravaas, Christ of Sauer, Tormod Engelsviken, Maqsood Kamil and Knud Jorgensen. Oxford: Regnum Books International, 2015.

Schnelle, Udo. *Apostle Paul: His Life and Theology*. Grand Rapids: Baker Academics, 2003.

Schoeps, H.J. *Paul: The Theology of the Apostle in the Light of Jewish Religious History*, translated by Harold Knight. Philadelphia: The Westminster Press, 1961.

Schreiner, T.R. "Works of the Law," in *DPL*. Illinois: InterVarsity Press, 1993.

Schreiner, Thomas R. *Paul.* Leicester: InterVarsity Press, 2001.

Schutz, J.H. *Paul and the Anatomy of Apostolic Authority*. Cambridge: Cambridge University Press, 1975.

Schweitzer, A. *The Mysticism of Paul the Apostle*, 2nd ed. London: A. & C. Black, 1953.

Schweitzer, Albert. *The Mysticism of Paul the Apostle*. New York: The Macmillan Co., 1955.

Scott, James C. *Domination and the Arts of Resistance, Hidden Transcripts*. London: Yale University Press, 1990.

Segal, A. F. *Paul the Convert: The Apostolate and the Apostasy of Saul the Pharisee*. London: Yale University Press, 1990.

Shannahan, Chris. *A Theology of Community Organizing: Power to the People.* New York: Routledge, 2014.

Shires, Henry M. *The Eschatology of Paul: In the Light of Modern Scholarship*. Philadelphia: The Westminster Press, 1946.

Singh, Nikky-Guninder Kaur. *Sikhism: An Introduction.* New York: I. B. Tauris, 2011.

Singh, Sardar Harjeet. *Faith and Philosophy of Sikhism.* Delhi: Kalpaz Publications, 2009.

Smith, Dennis E. *From Symposium to Eucharist: The Banquet in the Early Christian World.* Minneapolis: Fortress Press, 2003.

Smith, Gordon T. *A Holy Meal: The Lord's Supper in the Life of the Church*. Michigan: Baker Academics, 2005.

Sobanaraj, S. *Diversity in Paul's Eschatology: Paul's View on the Parousia and Bodily Resurrection.* Delhi: ISPCK, 2007.

Srinivas, M.N. *Caste in Modern India and Other Essays*. New Delhi: Asia Publishing House, 1962.

Standahl, Krister. *Paul among Jews and Gentile*. Philadelphia: Fortress Press, 1976.

Stanley, S. J. David Michael. *Christ Resurrection in Pauline Soteriology*. Romae: E. Pontificio Instituto Biblico, 1961.

Talbert, Charles H. *Ephesians and Colossians*. Michigan: Baker Academic, 2007.

Tcherikover, Victor. *Hellenistic Civilization and the Yews,* translated by S. Applebaum. New York: Atheneum, 1975.

Tenney, Merrill C. *Galatians: The Charter of Christian Liberty.* Michigan: William B. Eerdmans Publishing Company, 1989.

Theissen, Gerd. *Social Reality and the Early Christians: Theology, Ethics and the World of the New Testament,* translated by Margaret Kohl; Minneapolis, MN: Fortress Press, 1992.

Thomas, M.M. *Risking Christ for Christ's Sake: Towards an Ecumenical Theology of Pluralism*. Geneva: WCC Publications, 1987.

Thompson, James W. *Moral Formation According to Paul*. Grand Rapids, Michigan: Baker Academic, 2011.

Thompson, Marianne Meye. *Colossians and Philemon*. Michigan: William B. Eerdmans Publishing Company, 2005.

Tiede, David L. "Glory to Thy People Israel: Luke-Acts and Jews," in *Luke-Acts and Jewish People*, edited by Tyson. Philadelphia: Fortress Press, 1980.

Tucker, Christopher. "*Christology and the New Testament Jesus and His Earliest Followers.*" Edinburgh: University Press, 2001.

Vekathanam, Matthew "Source of Jewish-Christian Specificity Claims," *Religious Pluralism: An Introduction to Christian Perspective,* edited by Kuncheria Pathil. Delhi: ISPCK, 1999.

Victorinus, Stephen Cooper Marius. *Commentary on Galatians*. New York: Oxford University, 2005.

Vincent, Branick. *The House Church in the Writings of Paul*. Delaware: Michael Glazier Wilmington, 1989.

Waetjen, Herman C. *A Reordering of Power: A Socio-Political Reading of Mark's Gospel*. Minneapolis: Fortress Press, 1989.

Wahlstrom, Eric H. *The New Life in Christ*. Illinois: Muhlenberg Press, 1950.

Wainwright, Geoffrey. ed. *Keeping the Faith*. London: SPCK, 1989.

Watson, Paul F. *Paul, Judaism and the Gentiles: A Sociological Approach*. Cambridge: Cambridge University Press, 1986.

Webster, John C.B. *The Dalits Christians*: *A History*. New Delhi: ISPCK, 1994.

Wenham, David. *Paul: Follower of Jesus of Founder of Christianity?* Grand Rapids/Cambridge: William B. Eerdmans Publishing Company, 1995.

Whiteley, D.E.H. *The Theology of Paul*. Great Britain: Basil Blackwell, 1972.

Wright, N.T. *Paul and the Faithfulness of God*. Minneapolis: Fortress Press, 2013.

Wright, N.T. *Paul: In fresh Perspective*. Minneapolis: Fortress Press, 2005.

__________. *Theology of the New Testament*. Grand Rapids: William B. Eerdmans Publishing Company, 1974.

Yinger, Kent L. *The New Perspective on Paul: An Introduction*. Eugene, Oregon: Cascade Book, 2011.

C. Journal Articles

Bhattcharya, Amit "Unclaimed and Unredeemed: Gender, Marginality and Kamal Das' Poetics of Resistance," *Artha Journal of Social Sciences* 10/2 (July-December, 2011): 16.

Blair, E.P "Paul's Call to the Gentile Mission," *Biblical Research* 10 (1965): 19-33.

Blue, B.B. "Food Offered to Idols and Jewish food Laws," in *Dictionary of Paul and His Letters DPL* (Illinois: InterVarsity Press, 1993): 307.

Cosgrone, Charls H. "Justification in Paul: A Linguistic and Theological Reflection" *Journal of Biblical Literature* 106/4 (December, 1987): 653-670.

Dennison, William D. "Indicative and Imperative: The Basic Structure of Pauline Ethics" in *Calvin Theological Journal*, Vol. 14 (April 1979-November 1997): 58.

Drane, John W. "Tradition, Law and Ethics in Pauline Theology" in *Novum Testamentum*, Vol. XVI (January, 1974): 172.

Dunn, James D.G. "Ethos of Intra-Jewish Polemic in Paul's Letter to the Galatians" *Journal of Biblical Literature* 112/3 (Fall, 1993): 459-477.

__________. Whatever Happened to the Lord's Supper? *Epworth Review*. Vol. IX, No. 1 (January, 1992): 35.

__________. "The New Perspective on Paul," *BJRL* 65 (1983): 95-122.

__________. "The Incident at Antioch (Gal 2:11-18)," *JSNT* 18 (1983): 3-57.

Eastman, Susan "The Evil Eye and the Curse of the Law: Galatians 3.1 Revisited," *JSNT* 83 (2001): 69–87.

Elliott, John H. "Paul, Galatians, and the Evil Eye," *Cross Current in Theology and Mission* 17 (August, 1990): 262–271.

__________."Social-Scientific Criticism of the New Testament: More on Methods and Models," *Semeia* 35 (1986): 1.

Esler, Philip F. "Making and Breaking an Agreement Mediterranean Style: A New Reading of Galatians 2:1–14," *BibInt* 3 (1995): 285–314.

Fitzmyer, S. J. Joseph A. "The Letter to the Galatians," *NJBC*, 782.

Gundhy-volf, "Universalism," *DPL* 1:956.

Gupta, Nijay K. "James D.G. Dunn and the New Perspective on Paul: A Review Article," *Ashland Theological Journal* (2009): 137.

Hagopian, Rich "To be Right with God: An Exploration of the New Perspective View on Paul," *Ashland Theological Journal* (2005): 19.

Hall, Robert G. "The Rhetorical Outline for Galatians, a Reconstruction" *Journal of Biblical Literature* 106/2 (June, 1987): 277-287.

Horrell, D.G. "The Lord's Supper at Corinth and in the Church Today," *Theology* 98 (1995): 196-202.

Jathanna, O.V. "Religious Pluralism: A Theological Critique," *Bangalore Theological Forum* XXXI/2 (December, 1999): 2.

Jewett, R. 'The Agitators and the Galatians Congregation,' *New Testament Studies* 17 (1970-71): 204-206.

Lambrecht, Jan. "Transgressor by Nullifying God's Grace: A Study of Galatians 2: 1-18" *Biblica* 72/2 (1991): 217-236.

Meier, John P. "Biblical Reflection: The Conflict at Antioch (Gal 2:11-14)," *Mid-Stream* 35/4 (October, 1996): 472.

Mitchell, Margaret M. "Peter's Hypocrisy" and Paul's: Two "Hypocrites" at the Foundation of Earliest Christianity?" *New Testament studies* 58 (April, 2012): 213.

Neyrey, Jerome H. "Bewitched in Galatia: Paul and Cultural Anthropology," *CBQ* 50 (1988): 72–100.

Ninian Smart, "Soteriology," *ER* 13:418.

__________, *GLNT* 1:612.

Oommen, George. "Conversion in India: Ahistorical Appraisal with Reference to M.K. Gandhi's Response to Conversion," *BTF* 32/1 (June, 2000): 159.

Prokulski, Walently Jr. "Conversion of St. Paul," *Catholic Biblical Quarterly* 19/4 (October, 1957): 456.

Scroggs, R. *"Paul and the Eschatological Woman," JAAR* 40 (1972): 283-303.

Smith, Jeffery. "An Overview and Critique of the New Perspective on Paul's Doctrine of Justification: Part two-the New Perspective Critiqued (1)," *Reformed Baptist Theological Review 111.1* (January, 2006): 118.

Stendahl, K. 'The Apostle Paul and the Introspective Conscience of the West,' *Harvard Theological Review 56* (1963): 199-215.

Thomas, Robert L. "Hermeneutics of the New Perspective on Paul," *The Master Seminary Journal* 16/2 (Fall, 2005): 294.

Verseput, Donald. "Paul's Gentile Mission and the Jewish Christian Community Study of the Narrative in Galatians 1 and 2" *New Testament Studies* 39 (January, 1993): 36-58.

Wood, Irving F. "Paul's Eschatology," *JSTOE: The Biblical World* 38/2 (August, 1911): 79-91.

Wright, N.T. 'One God, One Lord, One People: Incarnational Christology for a Church in a Pagan Environment,' *Ex Auditu* 7 (1991): 45-58.

Newspaper

Deccan Herald, 21st December 2014.